Writing Music for Television and Radio Commercials

A Manual for Composers and Students

Michael Zager

THE SCARECROW PRESS, INC.
Lanham, Maryland, and Oxford
2003

SCARECROW PRESS, INC.

Published in the United States of America
by Scarecrow Press, Inc.
A wholly owned subsidiary of the Rowman & Littlefield Publishing Group, Inc.
4501 Forbes Boulevard, Suite 200, Lanham, MD 20706
www.scarecrowpress.com

PO Box 317
Oxford
OX2 9RU, UK

British Library Cataloguing in Publication Information Available

Library of Congress Cataloging-in-Publication Data

Zager, Michael.
 Writing music for television and radio commercials : a manual for composers and students / Michael Zager.
   p. cm.
 Includes index.
 ISBN 0-8108-4722-1 (pbk.)
 1. Television music—Instruction and study. 2. Radio music—Instruction and study. 3. Television advertising. 4. Radio
advertising. I. Title.
MT67 .Z34 2003
781.5'413—dc21

2002156067

∞ ™ The paper used in this publication meets the minimum requirements of American National Standard for Information Sciences—Permanence of Paper for Printed Library Materials, ANSI/NISO Z39.48-1992.
Manufactured in the United States of America.

*To my wife, Jane, our children, Jonathan, Allison, Stephen,
and Nicholas, our grandson, Jack, and my mother, Frances.
Thank you for your love, support, and patience.*

Contents

Preface

Writing Music for Television and Radio Commercials is intended to be an overview of the process. A separate book could be written about many of the subjects covered. The only things that can be taught about this creative process are the "tools" of composition and arranging and how to approach and analyze a creative situation. Applying these methods will help the composer achieve his creative goals. It is also important to realize that when dealing with advertising agencies the composer is immersed in a strange mixture of music and business. The advertising agency's goal is to please its client; pleasing the client means selling the product or creating an image for the client. It is the composer's job to help in this process, not necessarily to write what pleases the composer. The ideal is to be able to compose a piece of music that satisfies both the creative needs of the composer and the business objectives of the agency and the client.

It is advisable, but not necessary, for the student to have a basic knowledge of theory, harmony, and orchestration in order to gain the most from this book. There are many jingle writers who are successful without this knowledge; it is more unusual for a composer who specializes in underscoring (background music) not to have these skills. This book can be used in conjunction with the study of the above-mentioned courses and with the study of film scoring. Composing commercials is a unique craft and should be studied as a separate discipline. Advertising writers, art directors, and music producers can also use sections of this book to understand the creative process from a composer's point of view. Please note that the CD included with this book contains examples of various types of music and sound effects discussed in the text. When a CD track applies directly to what's being described in the book, you'll be directed to that specific track with a note enclosed in [brackets].

The course should be studied during two semesters, with an increasing level of complexity. The student should feel comfortable with tackling any potential assignment by the end of the second semester.

Acknowledgments

Without the mentoring, teaching, and friendship of David Tcimpidis of the Mannes College of Music, a division of New School University, this book would not have been written. Thank you for making my dream of becoming an educator a reality.

I would like to thank my friends, whose knowledge and expertise contributed to the information in this book. To my friend, first editor, and business agent, Robert Rainier—thank you for your guidance and for sharing your vast knowledge of music book publishing; to my colleagues Alfred Brown, Dr. Patricia Fleitas, Marshall Grantham, Joel Harrison, Dale Johnson, Lisa Kalb, Mark Mayhew, Arthur Meranus, Dr. Raul Murciano, Dennis Powers, and John Russo, thank you for sharing your years of experience with me.

I would like to thank my publisher, Scarecrow Press, and my editors, Bruce Phillips and Melissa Ray. And, finally, to my colleagues at Florida Atlantic University in Boca Raton: Dean William Covino, Dr. Heather Coltman, Dr. Lynn Appleton, Dr. Dorothy Leland, Dr. Rick Osburn, and Dr. Anthony Tamburri. Thank you for making every day seem like a *number-one hit*!

Introduction

A study by the *Harvard Business Review* concluded that people remember 20 percent of what they hear, 30 percent of what they see, and an astounding 70 percent of what they hear and see.

While the process of composing involves many steps and skills, the end result from the listener's standpoint is always some form of emotional reaction. When performed, music produces an emotional reaction in the listener. Therefore, when writing music for television and radio commercials, the composer must focus on producing this emotional reaction. Sometimes the audience might not even be aware of the music when viewing a commercial; however, if the music were removed, it would immediately be noticeable, and the entire audience response to the commercial could change. It is the job of the composer to achieve the emotional response that the creative team (writer, art director, and producer) wants to elicit. The music must enhance the scenes and add emotion to the message behind the concept of the commercial. *The music must help "tell the story."*

Throughout the decades, music has always held a special place among the arts because of the emotional response it creates. Throughout history, various cultures have banned music and thought of it as evil. People have been jailed for listening to and playing music; instruments have been burned. Songs have always reflected the attitudes and mores of society.

In Plato's *Republic*, Socrates wanted to ban the musical modes (specific scales) "because more than anything else rhythm and harmony find their way to the inmost soul and take strongest hold upon it, bringing with them an imparting grace, if one is rightly trained, and otherwise the contrary."

It is the emotional reaction one receives from hearing music that creates a lasting impression. For example, when a song is heard on the radio, a particular memory usually comes to mind. In the film *Jaws*, the two-note bass theme that was played when the shark was near created an anticipation of danger; on the Intel commercials, the musical logo (theme) at the end of the spots is anticipated, since the viewer has heard it so often; on the television program *The X-Files*, the short musical theme and unusual synthesizer sound playing that theme both create an emotional response and musically telegraph to the audience the general concept of the entire series.

Music can evoke any mood imaginable. The composer's choice of instruments, harmonic structure, compositional structure, recording techniques, and synthesizer effects all evoke an emotional response from the audience.

Commercials are tested before going on the air to get a sample audience's opinion of the music. Very often, if the music does not test well, the composer is asked to write a new composition. Sometimes, the creatives (writer and art director) want the "musical message" to change.

The subtlest compositional device can affect the audience's emotional response. For example, if the composer uses a negative-sounding musical sound effect with a scene that is supposed to provoke a positive response, the audience might have a negative reaction to the entire commercial. This is a common compositional problem, and the composer must be very clear about what mood the creative people want to achieve. The other problem is that musical effects and moods are subjective. What might sound interesting or positive to the composer might sound negative to the audience.

In contemporary society, virtually all forms of entertainment and information presentations use music, for example, commercials, motion pictures, television programs, industrial films and shows, corporate events, electronic games, recordings, and more. The emotional mood that music creates is of the utmost importance. For example, very often a specific style of music is heard when one is put on hold on a call to a business. When calling an airline, one usually hears "middle-of-the-road" music (sometimes with voice-over announcements), because the music has to appeal to a large demographic. When calling the Latin department of a record label, the caller will generally hear samples of their latest Latin releases. Not only does the music create a mood and image for a company, it also serves as an advertisement.

The right musical style can make the difference between success and failure. It is always advisable to have in-depth discussions with the creative people at the advertising agency, so that there is a clear understanding of the assignment and what has to be accomplished with the music. Even though most creatives (writers and art directors) have a clear vision of the role they want the music to play, it is advisable for the composer to have contributed additional suggestions. The composer is the expert, and the experienced creatives will generally consider the composer's input seriously.

1

Advertising Agency and Process Structure

HOW AN ADVERTISING AGENCY DEVELOPS COMMERCIALS FOR TELEVISION

Advertising agencies are the organizations that generally hire composers to write music for commercials. Clients hire agencies to plan, design, place, and supervise their advertisements or advertising campaigns. Not all agencies perform all functions; some agencies might only buy the media placement, while others might only create and execute the print, television, and radio commercials. Large agencies generally perform all these services.

Most global agencies provide additional services that are related to advertising, that is, public relations, direct marketing, sales promotion, and media buying. The large agencies must be full-service providers, in order to compete with their competition.

Since many of these agencies have international accounts, they must take into consideration the local culture of their consumer. This affects both the advertising and the music. Global agencies are very concerned with having international accounts because they can be lucrative and help to attract local clients. All large agencies must have both in order to remain in business.

For example, when one looks at the music charts throughout the world, the top ten records are never the same. If the agency decides to create a piece of original advertising music to be used on a worldwide basis and the assignment is to reflect current, popular worldwide musical culture, the agency creative people and the composer should search for international hits and use the feel and structure of the music as an example to emulate.

Since cultures vary, the agency might use the same music on a variety of different commercials that have been specifically designed for the local culture. Sometimes, the agencies will have different music on each commercial because they want it to reflect the local musical taste.

Most agencies are universally concerned about building a brand for their clients and servicing the consumer. The final result has to be either product sales or to successfully build a brand image. The music serves as a significant part of the creative process.

In general, after months of market research, the client provides the advertising agency with a list (referred to as a "laundry list") of marketing objectives they would like to achieve through advertising. Sometimes the agency is involved in choosing these objectives. In most modern agencies, the key creative, research, and account people will work with the client to plan the creative strategy that will best accomplish their business objectives. It is important for the composer to understand how the advertising business works, in order to create music that goes with the business strategy of a particular product. It is also necessary to understand the inner workings of an agency because the composer has to work within that structure.

The following is an actual creative brief ("laundry list") for a beauty product. This brief was given to the author before he composed the music. The name of the product has been withheld.

CREATIVE BRIEF FOR TELEVISION

Advertising Objective

1. To generate awareness and promote trial of (product name)
2. To drive the customer to the counter to purchase the product and/or receive a complimentary sample with a consultation on how to use the product

Target Audience

1. Forty-plus female users of facial treatment products who are concerned about the signs of aging
2. Women who want to reduce wrinkles

Customer Benefit

1. The product is a unique formula designed to reduce and correct the appearance of wrinkles.

Reason to Believe

1. The formula is patented by the manufacturer and delivers powerful, full-strength, anti-wrinkle benefits within the skin's surface layers. The targeted formula is time-released to fight wrinkles continuously for sixteen hours.
2. After two weeks: Fine lines begin to disappear, smoother skin is revealed.
3. After four weeks: Surface wrinkles are reduced, age spots fade, skin is visibly resurfaced.

Tone

1. Breakthrough, contemporary
2. Efficacious, scientific, technological

Executions

1. :30 television spot

Timing

1. Spot begins to air on November 19. (Tapes due to accounts beginning on October 19.)

This brief was given to all people connected to the account. It served as a guide for the writer, the composer, the director, the editor, the producer, and the account people.

DEMOGRAPHICS

Demographics is the study of human population. There is usually a choice when determining the potential marketing and advertising strategy for a product. One choice is to gear the advertising toward a particular demographic. The agency and client do extensive research to find their target market . Sometimes a well-thought-out strategy can open up new markets never before reached.

There are many companies doing this kind of research. Random phone calls are normally the first step; the purpose is to find the age group of their potential customers, the magazines people read, their income, the kind of cars they drive, what kind of music they like, and anything else that will provide a profile of the potential buyer. If an individual seems to fit the proper profile, they might be asked to attend a *focus group* for which they are paid a fee; people are selected at shopping centers, church groups, or any other source that could help provide relevant information.

Focus groups are held for the purpose of research before a creative strategy is developed; commercial ideas are sometimes tested before final production. Groups are of varying sizes, from one to two up to ten people. In a large group, some people might dominate the conversation, causing relevant information from the others to be missed. The agency might make a list of twenty or thirty potential "tag" lines (slogans) or show pictures that create a visual image of the product to see which ones get the best reaction from the participants.

The information from the various focus groups is compiled and a report given to the agency and client. This information is used as a guide to determine the kind of advertising and marketing that could appeal to their potential buyers.

> Example of a demographic: Women between the ages of eighteen and twenty-two; women with ambition who plan to have business careers, which denotes that they are generally intelligent people.

PSYCHOGRAPHICS

Psychographics is the study of psychological reasons people do things. There are many products for which the demographic of the buyer does not matter; the product is supposed to solve a psychological problem or concern. For example, there are people who go to health food stores to buy special vitamins because they want to stay healthy. Some of these buyers earn twenty thousand dollars a year, while others may earn one hundred thousand dollars a year. Their ages might range from twenty to seventy-five, and their gender is irrelevant. The advertising is geared toward their health issues or emotional needs rather than toward a specific age or income group. The purpose of the advertising is to address a need.

> Example of Psychographics: For many years, Clairol (the beauty care company) used the popular slogan "Does she . . . or doesn't she?" Now they have changed their entire focus and are using the slogan "Clairol, a beauty all your own" for all of their hair color products. Their intention is to convey the message that beauty comes in all forms. They are not targeting people of a specific age or weight or people who belong to any other particular group. The message is that beauty is individual; there is not just one standard. This is the first time in fifty years that Clairol is focusing on overall image rather than on individual products.
>
> The results of their research showed that women are rejecting one beauty standard that is primarily conveyed through advertising; also, attitudes toward aging and multiculturalism have changed. One of their print ads shows a picture of eleven happy looking women of various ages, ethnicities, and hair colors, with the slogan "a beauty all their own" across the picture.
>
> Even though Clairol's products are geared toward women, this is a good example of psychographical advertising.

HOW RESEARCH AFFECTS MUSIC

The results from demographic and psychographic research affect the style of music that should be used for the commercials. In the case of a specific demographic, if the research shows that the average buyer is twenty to thirty years old and female, the agency would most likely suggest music that appealed to that age bracket. In the case of psychographic research, the music must not offend any of the many groups that might buy the product. Therefore, the agency would probably want music that is not intrusive or too identifiable to a specific group. Of course, this is a generalization; creatives might try many approaches and go in the direction opposite the one that would be most acceptable by traditional standards. For instance, there are forms of contemporary music that appeal to a diverse demographic. It is a good idea for the composer to make creative suggestions at the appropriate time.

THE PROCESS OF DEVELOPING ADVERTISING

After analyzing the results of the research, the creative department will then work on numerous ideas for advertising campaigns or individual commercials. The creative director will generally pick several strong ideas for development and presentation to the client.

After the client has selected the campaigns or individual commercials they feel will best portray the message they are trying to deliver to their target audience, the agency will generally test these ideas with focus groups. Focus groups comprise average people in the proper target market, who are paid to view some form of presentation of the commercial(s), give feedback, and be willing to be interviewed.

Most creative ideas for television commercials are presented to clients and focus groups (following the initial focus group sessions, which concentrate on exploratory questions) either in storyboard form or through the use of animatics or steal-o-matics.

A *storyboard* consists of a group of photographs or cartoon-type drawings with dialogue and/or voice-over copy written under each frame; visual instructions, such as camera angles, lighting, and any other essential descriptive information, are also included. The "story" of the commercial is displayed.

An *animatic* is basically a "moving" storyboard. The board is usually shot on video, with dialogue or voice-over added. Very often, a composer is hired to add music. Animatics give the client and focus groups a very good idea of what the final film will look like. Some animatics portray a feeling of movement.

A *steal-o-matic* comprises a series of scenes taken from film libraries, old movies, television shows, commercials, and any other video source with appropriate footage; these scenes are edited together in such a way that they look like the commercial the agency proposes to film. This is the most realistic visualization of how the commercial would look. Many times, when the audio, including the music, is added to a steal-o-matic, it appears complete enough to be aired, but this is impossible, because the rights to most of the film are not available. The agency takes the risk of making the steal-o-matic look *too* good, because some of the scenes could be expensive to film. Therefore, it is possible that the final agency film might not look as good as the demo.

> Limited Productions: In rare instances, agencies produce limited productions, which are scaled-down versions of the commercial, using actors, music, voice-overs, and any other elements that will make the spot look as complete as possible, while spending much less money than the budget allows. The production is then tested in a focus group or on television in a limited market. If the commercial(s) tests well, the agency will do a full production.

Usually, the commercials that obtain the highest focus group scores are produced and aired. Some agencies give great importance to focus group scores, while others use the results as a part of the overall puzzle. The winning presentation is eventually given to the director to use as a guide for filming.

The focus group participants are asked many questions concerning the commercials, including what their reaction is to the music. The composer may be asked to rewrite the music if the focus group reaction is poor.

> During the initial research phase, the focus group participants are asked questions that will help the researchers develop a profile of their potential buyers. The agency might present a series of "tag" lines, which could eventually become the most identifiable slogan connecting the public to the product, or visual images might be presented and explored. This could help the creatives take the proper approach to developing a campaign and image for the product.

Many products and commercials are tested in a specific region of the United States. If the product sells, the commercial or campaign is considered successful and airtime is bought on a national basis, assuming the product is sold nationally.

> Some products, although sold nationally, have the majority of sales in a particular region of the country. In this case, the greatest share of the media buying takes place in that region. For example, the majority of sales for Dr Pepper are in the Western and Southwestern parts of the United States, and therefore, most of the commercials for Dr Pepper are aired in those areas.

Companies spend substantial amounts of money testing ideas and campaign concepts before any commercials are completed. The client and the agency must feel relatively secure that the basic concept and message they are trying to communicate will be successful. The agency people, both creative and business, make sure that every frame of picture, dialogue, and/or voice-over that was approved in the test presentation is replicated in the final filming by the director.

Sometimes, the process of planning advertising involves months of presentations and revisions before anything is presented on television. Most of the time, the radio commercials mirror the television commercials. (Radio commercials do not usually receive the same amount of preparation and investigation as television commercials because they are usually extensions of the television campaigns.)

THE FUNCTION OF MUSIC IN ADVERTISING

Music provides an important ingredient in the creative process. A well-crafted composition can create an identity for a product. Some of the most memorable advertising slogans are used as lyrics in advertising jingles (short songs).

> Some examples of advertising slogans used as lyrics in jingles are "G.E., we bring good things to life," "The Pepsi generation," and "Come see the softer side of Sears."

Advertising Age, a leading trade magazine, listed what they thought were the ten most effective slogans of the twentieth century. Many have been the basis for jingles:

1. Diamonds are forever (DeBeers)
2. Just do it (Nike)
3. The pause that refreshes (Coca-Cola)
4. Tastes great, less filling (Miller Lite)
5. We try harder (Avis)
6. Good to the last drop (Maxwell House)
7. Breakfast of champions (Wheaties)
8. Does she . . . or doesn't she? (Clairol)
9. When it rains it pours (Morton Salt)
10. Where's the beef? (Wendy's)

The following are honorable mentions:

1. Look Ma, no cavities! (Crest toothpaste)
2. Let your fingers do the walking (Yellow Pages)
3. Loose lips sink ships (public service)
4. M&Ms melt in your mouth, not in your hand (M&M candies)
5. We bring good things to life (General Electric)

Musical logos are identifiable short melodies usually played at the end of a commercial or used as a symbol for a product or company. Probably the most recognizable musical logo is for NBC Television; just three notes created a network identity that has lasted for many years.

> Most television networks and individual stations hire advertising agencies to create the promotions for their shows (TV print and radio) and to help create an image for individual stations and networks. A musical example is the use of the John Williams's theme for all NBC News events. When the audience hears the NBC theme, there is an automatic subliminal reaction that lets them know that they are going to view something associated with NBC News.

Underscoring is the background music used behind dialogue, voice-overs, film, or video. This musical form can provide the ambience for an entire commercial. There are quite a few commercials that have no dialogue and use only pictures and music.

When an agency makes a "pitch" to a client for a campaign or individual commercials, a creative strategy is presented, and within that strategy is a reference to music. They might suggest that the music be fun, authoritative, serious, or warm, or that it evoke an emotion that supports the advertising. Sometimes, musical examples will be played at the meeting—a composer might be asked to record a demo in a certain style, or something from a commercial CD might be presented as an example. There are no rules.

THE MUSIC PRODUCER'S ROLE

Because of the important role that music plays in commercials, agencies pay very close attention to the content of the music and the production of the music. Some agencies (mainly large companies) have music producers, whose job is to produce advertising music for the agency.

Music production in advertising is similar to producing records or producing music for motion pictures. The best analogy is to compare it to the process of film direction. The film director is responsible for the creative quality of the final film, and the music supervisor is responsible for the production and quality of the music. The music producer in advertising is responsible for the final music presentation. The job requires the music producer to make sure that:

1. The music meets the needs of the creative team. The creative team is generally specific about the musical needs of a commercial(s). The advertising producer is responsible for the end product.
2. The sound quality and musicianship are of the highest standard.
3. The synchronization of the music to the film is correct. If during the recording session the producer feels that the music has to be adjusted to match the film, it is the producer's responsibility to deal with the composer.
4. The highest technical standards of the industry are met.

The music producer also helps select the proper composer for the particular job. Demonstration reels of various composers are presented to the creatives, who are usually searching for a certain style of music. In most cases, the composer who has compositions closest to what the creatives want gets the assignment. Additionally, the music producer puts together music production budgets and residual payment estimates.

Musicians and singers receive recording session fees for the initial recording. *Residual payments* are additional fees paid to musicians and singers (actors and announcers) based on the amount of airplay a commercial receives and on the number of markets in which it is shown. The residual payment scale is negotiated among the musicians' and singers' unions and representatives from the advertising industry.

Residuals are not paid in all states of the United States. For example, Texas and Florida are considered right-to-work states and are nonunion states. The payments paid to musicians and singers in nonunion states are called "buyouts." This means they get a one-time payment for their services and do not receive residual payments or union benefits.

Sometimes, the account supervisor, or account executive, will attend the music recording session to "hand hold" the clients, who usually do not understand the recording process. For that reason, the composer should try to have as few surprises in the studio as possible. In order to lower the risk of encountering problems while in the recording studio, a music demonstration, known as a demo, is almost always requested by the agency and then approved by the client before the final music is produced.

THE COMPOSER'S ROLE

In most cases, the composer is the last person to be hired to complete the production of a commercial, because when music is added as an underscoring (background music), it is essential that the composer view the final, edited picture in order to write music that will enhance it. Unless the client has approved the final edit, the music will most likely have to be rewritten; changing the edit will change the placement of the music. It is also possible that the meaning of the picture could change, depending on how the film has been edited. This could affect the direction and style of the music.

> Example of a typical problem in television commercials: If the music is building to a powerful musical "hit" (music and picture happening simultaneously) and the section of film has been moved back by four frames, the audience will hear the "hit" too early. The rule of thumb is that the audience can hear and see a variable of two frames of picture. If the section of film is varied more than that, not only will the "hit" be perceived as being early, but also the music following it will not be in sync. This is why it is essential for the composer to ask if what was presented is the final edited film. In reality, clients request editing changes numerous times before the final approved edit.

Sometimes, the composer is asked to write music prior to filming. The following are some of the reasons:

1. If singing or dancing is shown on camera, it is best to write and record the music prior to production. This way, the music track can be used on the set to help the singers and dancers achieve exact synchronization.

   > Suggestion: In the situation described in number 1, it is advisable for the composer to *suggest* that music be written and recorded before filming. The technical pitfalls of not doing this might not occur to the creatives. It is not uncommon to notice bad lip synching (singers moving their lips to a prerecorded track) and dancers not in time with the music. There are several reasons for this: 1) the singers did not lip-synch to the final music track during filming, 2) the director was not paying enough attention to the lip synching and to making sure the dancers were in time with the music during filming, and 3) bad editing. Most scenes are filmed numerous times, using various camera angles; if they are not edited properly and some of the selected scenes have synch problems, the end result is bad.

2. An alternative to the method described in number 1 is to record a simple melody with a click track tempo (a metronome click) and play that music track on the set while filming. This gives the singers and dancers the correct tempo. After the film has been edited and approved by the client, the final musical arrangement can then be completed. Sometimes, this is a preferred working method, because if changes are made during the filming, it is easier for the composer to adjust the final music track.

   > If the director wants the singers to sing live on the set, the music should not be prerecorded. This gives the singers the ability to create a more spontaneous, live performance. The sound engineer has to be very careful not to play the music track too loudly on the set, or the music will leak onto the vocal track and cause technical problems for the composer; this is called *leakage*. After the film has been completed, the composer receives a copy of the singing track and creates the final arrangement around the filmed vocals.
   >
   > The author had an unusual experience. The agency creatives decided that they wanted the actress in their commercial to sing the musical "tag" (an identifiable singing logo at the end of the spot). They were going to have her sing "wild," meaning without any musical track to guide her, which could have resulted in many problems: 1) There was a specific number of seconds allowed for the singing, and if the actress went over that time, the song would not have fit in the spot; 2) the key had to match the rest of the underscoring, so there would be a smooth transition; and 3) without guidance, the actress might not have sung the melody accurately. Because of logistical problems, the singer could not attend a separate recording session, so the tag had to be recorded on the set. A temporary piano track was looped (repeated) numerous times on a DAT (Digital Audio Tape), so the singer had an opportunity to sing and record the tag numerous times. The vocal was then separated from the piano track and added to the final music. The result was perfect, but the client decided to change the ending, so the actress eventually had to rerecord the vocal. Warning: Do not use cassettes to tape music, because their speed is not accurate.

3. Music is played on the set to help create an appropriate mood for the actors. Even with a presentation of only a storyboard, a musical background can help sell an idea to the client.

STRUCTURE OF THE CREATIVE TEAM AT AN ADVERTISING AGENCY

The composer deals directly with producers, writers, and art directors. (Writers and art directors are referred to as the "creatives.") The creatives are usually very specific about the musical direction of a commercial or campaign. The following are their job descriptions.

Advertising Producer

There are two kinds of advertising producers. One is an administrative producer, and the other is both administrative and creative. Producers calculate budgets and help find and hire the director, the composer, the editor, the announcer, and the actors, along with any other people necessary to accomplish an assignment. The important decisions have to be approved by the writer, the art director, the group creative director (the immediate supervisor of the writer and art director), and the agency creative director (the leading creative job at an agency); the agency will then make recommendations to the client and seek their approval before proceeding. While on location, the producers and the creative team supervise and are responsible for the entire production.

The following is my interview with Lisa Kalb, advertising producer:

Question: "What does an advertising producer do?"

Lisa: "A producer works with the creative team, the copywriter, and the art director in making their storyboard come to life, assisting them both creatively and financially—they are 100 percent responsible for the budget. The producer will help them find the director, the editor, and the music company, the right casting director, the right talent, does talent negotiating—negotiates rights maybe with a business manager, and is the liaison to the account team, the client, the creative team, and really works in consort with all of the players that I mentioned to make a commercial happen. From the minute a storyboard is handed to them to the moment it gets on the air, the producer is in charge of every stage of development."

Question: "Do you usually handle more than one job at a time?"

Lisa: "Not usually. Usually there is one big job and maybe five small jobs. There are a lot of commercials that music is redone for, reedited, or there are radio spots that need to be done, or there is bidding out many other jobs for future work, so there are always a number of other projects happening simultaneously, but some producers are fortunate enough to have assistants, some producers are unfortunate enough to have five big jobs going at the same time, so it varies."

Question: "Whom does a producer report to?"

Lisa: "It could be the head of production for the agency, or it could be the creative directors."

Question: "How much input does the average producer have on who gets hired to work on a commercial?"

Lisa: "If it is a good experienced producer who has a good track record with the agency and specifically with the creatives, the producer might have a great relationship with the creative director or just with the art director on the team. If that is all in place, I would say my input is pretty well accepted and important, and I would say anywhere between 50 and 75 percent in my particular case. The norm is that the producer is not part of the creative team. The more unusual situation is when the producer is brought in to offer creative solutions. I have been asked to devise storyboards based on how it will affect production."

Question: "I have worked with producers who have no creative input. Is that unusual?"

Lisa: "I would say it's common. I'd say it's fifty-fifty. For example, it depends upon how strongly a copywriter or an art director feels about an area of expertise in a commercial. In the area of music, the copywriter or the art director more often than not have a specific point of view. I would say music is the area in which—for myself— my opinion might be less taken. In the area of music, I'd say the creative teams really rule."

Question: "Do producers specialize in certain types of productions?"

Lisa: "Absolutely. I am beauty [production]. There are producers who just work on cars. Retail is an area, knowing how to tag [change endings] hundreds and hundreds of versions a year . . . that's a specialty, and there are many nuances involved with that . . . in just cranking out and knowing how to get the best prices."

Question: "Do freelance producers usually market themselves in one area?"

Lisa: "No, they shouldn't. It's too limiting. There are so few jobs out there, and if you are lucky, you are going to be able to be working on many different things, so that you can have a number of different types of works on your reel and you can keep selling yourself in any area."

Question: "How often does the style of the final music end up being what the creatives first envisioned?"

Lisa: "I'd say 25 percent of the time the original style of music, as directed, is accepted in the end."

Question: "What advice can you give to composers who want to compose advertising music?"

Lisa: "Versatility is really great, or just being really fabulous doing one particular style of music. That way you can freelance and work for a number of different music companies, with them knowing that you are an expert in one particular style of music. If you want to have your own music company, you do need to be versatile. Work for someone for a number of years is the best advice, because it's really hard."

Not all agencies afford the producer the same responsibilities and authority. At some agencies the producers are part of a production department, and at other agencies the producers are part of the creative department. If there are problems, the producer consults with the head of production. At some agencies the producers report to the production head, while at other agencies they work directly for the creative director. Let us assume that the shoot is running over budget and the creative team wants to keep shooting because they do not feel that the director has captured their vision. The final decision is made based on the hierarchy at the agency; in some agencies the head of production has the final power, and at others the creative director has it. A representative from the client is always at a filming and will ultimately give permission to go over budget.

Example: (Television Commercials) Many directors think that they can improve the commercial that the client has approved for filming. The smart directors will film what the client has approved and then ask permission to shoot an alternative version. The key word is *ask*. There are many directors who will not be rehired by an agency because they refuse to shoot the approved commercial.

Copywriter

Copywriters and art directors are usually teamed together to create and develop advertising concepts; the creative director gives the writer and art director specific instructions as to the objectives of the client. A copywriter's primary job is to write scripts, announcers' copy, and print copy.

Here is my interview with Joel Harrison, who is a copywriter and creative director:

Question: "What does a copywriter do?"

Joel: "The basic job of a copywriter is to communicate the benefits of a product or service to the prospective buyer—the viewer on television, the reader of any printed material, the listener of the radio—and to do it in a creative, compelling, riveting way so it's not boring. The worst thing a copywriter can do in advertising is to write boring copy."

Question: "When an agency hires a copywriter, are they expected to write print as well as broadcasting, or are some copywriters specialists?"

Joel: "These days since there is so much television, you get into the advertising business as even a cub copywriter, you'll write television as well as print—moreover, more and more advertising is over the Internet, so there are even more kinds of media these days for copywriters to get involved with."

Question: "Do you think that the Internet will become a major source of sales as a result of advertising on the Internet?"

Joel: "It's really the future. I think there will be new forms of advertising. I think that over time, we will be seeing less and less advertising on television, certainly network television and even cable television. I think there is going to be more one on one—a certain advertiser will find out where they can reach his or her main prospect for buying a product, and they will try and get that message to that person. A lot is going to be done on the Internet. I can see more and more of an advertiser's message being directed that way."

Question: "How are commercials created?"

Joel: "It is almost always a team effort—a writer and an art director working together on an assignment. I as a creative director will decide who I want working on it, depending upon the importance of the project, we would all sit down in a room—the account people, strategic planners [and the creative team]—they will have found out who the target audience is, what the benefit of the product or service is, and key consumer insight—where our head should be in trying to come up with some successful and compelling copy to sell the product. That's the way it is done—give the assignment to a team or several teams, set up a timetable, probably work backwards from when the advertising has to air or be in print."

Referring to the creative work, Joel Harrison says: "Any good creative director won't just say they don't like the work, they will say, "Hey, you've got a great selling line here, why don't you try it this way? Why don't you try doing it with music? Try doing it with a testimonial approach." That's what a creative director does—gives creative direction. I know plenty of creative directors who just look at work and say this stinks. You've got to tell them why you don't think it is hitting the mark, why you don't think it's a bull's-eye, what's wrong with it, what can be right with it."

Question: "How many campaigns do you develop for a presentation?"

Joel: "I always have had a rule of thumb. I would never show too much or too little. I usually try to show two or three different ideas, and sometimes those two or three ideas may have several executions in them."

Question: "When you are working at a large agency, and you have your two or three ideas, what is the next step?"

Joel: "In a large agency, more times than not, you would then go to the executive creative director and then share it with the top account person. It's very important for the agency to have everybody on the same page, so you don't go to a client and there are any internal disagreements."

Question: "How much does the head account person have to say about the actual creative work as opposed to the content of the work?"

Joel: "It really varies. I find that really good account people get it. They understand where the creative heads are, because they've got a streak of creativity in their bodies themselves. I have had more than a few experiences where I have worked with account people who were so good that they sometimes have either come up with a creative idea or really enhanced it."

Question: "How does a person become a copywriter?"

Joel: "Put together a portfolio and take it to agencies. That will be your proof to them that 'I can do stuff, and I'm pretty good.'"

Question: "How do you decide on the kind of music you want for a commercial?"

Joel: "I can only speak for myself, but I think that whenever I have done something and I think it requires music, I've just come up with—in my head—what I think the music should be. But it is never that definitive, because I am not a musical expert—you or people like you are the music mavens. I would sit down and share ideas with you, give you input on how I hear it, and sometimes you would say, 'That won't work,' or you'd say, 'That's a terrific approach, let me mull that over and come up with a couple of ideas.' A lot of it is really gut."

Question: "How often do composers come up with music that is in a different direction than what you asked for?"

Joel: "Probably half of the time—a music person who just executes what I have in my head without coming up with something else is not really doing their job."

Question: "What percentage of copywriters know how to write lyrics, and how open are they to having the music company creating a lyric out of what you give them?"

Joel: "I have found that most copywriters don't know how to write [lyrics]. They can write lines, they may not scan, they may not work musically. It has been my experience that when you then take it to a good music company [they] in a very frank, open kind of discussion can point out things, point out ways of making it better. Sometimes they take the lyric and rewrite it. Sometimes they say, 'This won't work.' I have found that copywriters who write lyrics are not lyricists. They're not paid to be lyricists. Egos should not stand in the way of changing lyrics to make them better."

Question: "What do you do when you are handed a 'laundry list' of points to be included in a lyric and there is way too much information to fit into the short time span of a lyric for a commercial?"

Joel: "The advertising shouldn't start until there is an agreed-upon strategy, and that strategy should be very, very single-minded. An example is, 'Tasty Cakes taste great.' The reason for that is they have more butter and they are baked longer. That's a simplified strategy. If account people say that 'you have to say that we have been in business since 1923 and our ovens are made of iron and our delivery men have nicer mustaches and our icing has more sugar in it, then you are going to have advertising that is not going to work on any level. I am a big believer in less is more. A simplified strategy, whether you're doing a musical jingle or not, will lead to better, single-minded, stronger, and more successful advertising. If that [the simple strategy] doesn't contain the kitchen sink, you're not going to have to put in a lyric or a print ad."

Question: "What are some of the large national accounts you have worked on?"

Joel: "Lots of Proctor and Gamble business, Crest Toothpaste, Bounce, Dawn, Charmin, Ivory Snow, Zest, Craft General Foods, Cool Whip, Post Raisin Brand, Crystal Light, Texaco."

Question: "Do you find that copywriters specialize in categories?"

Joel: "I think these days that's true. The best example I can give you is Business to Business and the Internet. There are people who have training in that they started by working on World Com., or American Express. People like that become well versed in those categories. So I think it's very hard for someone who is working on, say, package goods, for example, to make the jump into something that is highly technical like the Internet and a lot of Business to Business advertising."

Question: "The advertising business is interesting because it is as much business as it is creative. My question is when you're creating an ad, are you thinking as a creative writer, are you thinking as a businessperson? What goes through your mind?"

Joel: "Yes, yes. More as a creative person because that's what they pay me to do, but I also think of it in terms of the business. I think of the category, I think of the competition, I think of what the competition is doing, how the competition will react to this, how we can beat the competition. I'm a big believer in knowing the business of advertising in addition to the creative side of advertising."

Question: "There are many creative commercials that are not good advertising. Can you give me some examples?"

Joel: "In the boom period of the Internet, some of the most creative and entertaining, most clever advertising was done for lots of the Internet companies, but most of them failed. They didn't burst the Internet bubble by themselves, but people were entertained by the advertising but had no idea whose company it was, and this is borne out by research. Any good, successful advertising will really connect the message to the product."

Question: "Is there any advice you would like to give to young composers who are going into the field of writing music for commercials?"

Joel: "I would say, listen to the creative people when you meet with them, but don't be afraid, don't be intimidated by them. Be strong. If you've got a good idea, don't keep it to yourself, don't be afraid of offending them, because if they have anything going for them, they will listen. These creative people are really not music people, they may have some instincts, as I alluded to before, but when you get into that room, you're going to size up pretty quickly what could be the right and best solution. Don't be afraid for a give and take, because in so many cases, they listen to you . . . you're the mavens, be strong, be bold, and don't be afraid."

Art Director

Art directors work with writers to create advertising concepts for both print and broadcasting. Art directors are responsible for the overall visual "look" of the commercial. Most commercials are first portrayed in a series of drawings called storyboards, which are either drawn or supervised by the art director. Each frame (picture) of the commercial is drawn and has visual and audio instructions (dialogue, visual, and audio effects, etc.) below each drawing. A well-drawn storyboard is usually a very close visualization of how the final film will look.

After the writer and the art director have presented an idea to their superiors and the idea has been accepted, the art director usually oversees the visual part of the presentation to the client.

The following is my interview with Arthur Meranus, art director and creative director:

Question: "What does an art director do?"

Arthur: "An art director usually works with a copywriter. When you are talking about newspaper advertising, the art director actually lays out the ad's position elements, supervises photography, the typography, and works with the writer to come up the most cogent advertising possible. In television, the art director works more as a storyboard artist. They work with a writer to develop an idea and then transfer that idea to a storyboard. Most often they will supervise the production of the television commercial. Art directors usually have some graphic design training, go to art school."

Question: "How much influence does the art director have in choosing music for a commercial?"

Arthur: "Generally, the art director, by definition, would not have a great deal of influence, but in today's business the art director is more of a jack of all trades and is really responsible, with the writer, for the creative product in total. So, his opinion and the writer's opinion weigh about equally in choosing music for commercials."

Question: "How do you choose the style of music for a commercial?"

Arthur: "If you want to have a continuing theme for the music, then you're dealing with multiple styles, and you pick the styles that seem to fit the situation that you're developing now. When it comes to designing [music] for a campaign, you have to make a decision whether you want it to sound very current or you want it to feel like a period piece, or do you want the music to drive the action, you want the music to be a bed for the action—how you deal with lyrics—all depend on the message and the tone of the advertising. So, most often you agree in advance what the tone of the advertising should be and then pick music to go with that tone."

Question: "How often does the initial musical direction end up being the musical style?"

Arthur: "Most often a good creative team will go to a music company with a tone and a feeling that they want to achieve, and then they will ask the music company if they have any ideas that fit their basic direction and if the music people come up with a better idea, a smart creative team will go along with that. I would say that happens one-third to one-half of the time."

STRUCTURE OF THE ACCOUNT TEAM AT AN ADVERTISING AGENCY

Account Directors, Account Supervisors, and Account Executives

The account people are the direct liaisons from the agency to the client and are involved in every area of client services.

They are the liaison to the media buying department (assuming that the agency buys the media for the client), which includes television, radio, newspaper, print, Internet, billboards, and any other form of advertising and marketing the client desires.

The agency receives commissions or fees for their services. (Fees are becoming a more popular form of compensation.)

Media placement is one of the most crucial functions of an agency. The wrong strategy can mean failure.

> Some agencies only provide the creative work, while others only provide the media buying. Most large agencies offer both services.

Researchers

Researchers help the client research the best advertising strategies to achieve their business goals. This involves extensive research.

> Some agencies are asked to help the client "invent" new product ideas. They find out what people need that is not available; the client will then develop a product to fit that need.
>
> The author has written music for fictional products; the labels and commercials have been developed as if the product existed. Sometimes, this work is tested to see if it is worth spending millions of dollars in development.
>
> For many years prescription drugs were not advertised to the public; now the purpose of this kind of advertising is for doctors to become aware of new medications and for patients to ask for it.

ASSIGNMENTS

1. Give an example of a product that has a demographic audience. State the demographic target and make several suggestions relating to the style of music that would appeal to that group. Write one or two pieces of music in the appropriate style.
2. Give an example of a psychographic audience. State the target audience and make several suggestions relating to the style of music that would appeal to that group. Write one or two pieces of music in the appropriate style.
3. Refer to the briefing (Creative Brief for Television) earlier in this chapter. Write two instrumental pieces, in different styles, that would accomplish the objectives. Explain the reasoning behind each approach.

2

Composing for Television and Radio Commercials vs. Composing for Films

Let me begin by saying this: Some commercials would not work if they contained music. Especially spots that depend on drama and tension—or are intended to be very serious.

Other spots call for sound design, which is not really music per se. But it's been my experience over the years that music can really be a driving force in making commercials work.

For years I created lots of vignette spots and used whimsical music tracks to tie the spots together and make them move. They were usually instrumental tracks but sometimes used lyrics.

Good, strong, stirring anthem-type spots—usually corporate in nature—can elevate a client's message, make it memorable and give viewers chills up and down their spine, which is a very good thing to happen!

Many highly successful spots don't contain one word of copy (incidentally, I as a copywriter, created such spots and didn't feel left out because it's really the idea that counts)—but rather, rely solely on great, mind-sticking music.

Bottom line: Music, when used well, written by composers who understand the role of advertising, can make a good spot better and turn a great spot into an award winner—and quite possibly a classic. I cannot emphasize enough the role music plays in broadcast advertising. So much so that sometimes the element people remember about a commercial is the music. Not the idea. But I guess, even then, if the music helps them remember the product—and they go out and buy the product—the clients haven't wasted their advertising dollars.

—Joel Harrison, former senior vice president and group creative director at DMB&B

The crafts of composing, orchestrating, and arranging are different for commercials than they are for films. Commercials are sometimes thought of as small films. All of the musical elements that are included in a film are included in commercials, but they must be accomplished in a much shorter period of time. The average film score has about forty minutes of music; the average television commercial lasts thirty seconds. This, obviously, is a drastic difference.

DIFFERENCES

Films: The director is the creative force. The film director usually hires the composer and gives the creative direction for the musical score. Most directors or editors will lay in temporary music to the film while editing. This music is referred to as a "temp score." The music from temp scores can come from any source, for example, CDs, music from other films, symphony recordings, and so forth. The purpose of the temp score is to give the director, producer, and composer a sense of the kind of music that will work with the film. The composer is then given the film with the temp score so he can refer to it while composing.

Some directors will want the original music to be in the exact style as the temp score, whereas others will tell the composer to use the temp score as a guide; all directors work differently. Most directors will want to hear a demo of each film cue (music session), which is usually accomplished by scoring the cues on synthesizers. The director can then make comments, and the composer can make changes before the final recording session.

13

Commercials: The copywriter, the art director, and some producers are the creative forces. Music for commercials is "music by committee." The composer is usually working with a creative team, and that team plus the agency creative director and the client must approve the final music. Sometimes this creates a problem, because the creative people might like different kinds of music and might have different conceptions as to the style of music that works best for the project. When there is disagreement, it is usually the executive creative director of the agency that makes the final decision.

> Some large agencies have music departments. The music producers guide the composer and act as the intermediary with the creative department. The approval of the final music almost always rests with the client.

Commercials: The ultimate approval comes from the client. Success is, usually, measured in increased sales and awareness of the product. Clients work in different ways—some rely on the agency creative director to pick the music; others want final approval on all aspects of the commercial. If there is a difference of opinion between the client and the agency, the agency will usually back up their suggestions with research and then look to the client to make the final decision.

> If the client does not see tangible results from the agency's work, they put the account up for review. This means that they invite several agencies to "pitch" the account. Each agency is given a budget and given a certain amount of time to present their creative and media buying ideas to the client.

Some large clients will only hire global agencies (worldwide offices), because they want a universal coordinated effort. Some clients also want an agency that is strong in media buying. Placing advertising (broadcasting and print) is both an art and a crucial business decision. Sometimes a client will hire one agency to do the creative work and another to buy the media. Some very large clients actually buy their own media, but this is rare.

Films: Studio heads make the final decisions. Success is measured at the box office. Very few directors have the right to the "final cut" (final edit). Major films are tested with audiences in much the same way that commercials are tested with focus groups. If there are problems, sometimes the director is asked to reshoot certain scenes or reedit. Directors will sometimes shoot two endings and test both.

In both films and commercials, music and sound (sound effects and dialogue) serve a vital function. If the music and sound are taken out of a film, most films will lose a vital part of their effectiveness. Music and effects are crucial to the emotional content of the film.

> In describing his art, Walter Munch, Academy Award winner for sound design for *The Godfather*, *The Conversation*, and *Apocalypse Now*, said, "Go to the art library and take out a book of paintings. Then go to the music library and try to choose music that stretches the point of a particular painting as far as it can be stretched."

As previously stated, the main difference between television and radio commercials and film writing is the length of the compositions. A commercial music writer composes pieces that run between ten seconds and one minute. Within that time period, there could be many visual and emotional changes that have to be addressed within the composition. Sometimes the music can be one theme with a varied orchestration that conforms to the changes in the pictures. Changes can occur within a second or two. In other instances, one commercial may require numerous musical styles and themes; for example, a commercial showing various ports of call for a ship line may require music indigenous to each country referenced.

> It is common for a commercial to have a completely different mood in the first half than in the second. Typical would be a commercial for a pain reliever such as aspirin. The beginning of the commercial might portray someone with a headache, who by the end, after taking the product, is pain-free. The music must enhance the different messages of the pictures.

The most difficult skill to master is to make the composition sound cohesive rather than like numerous disjointed musical sections. This skill is developed through the use of compositional and arranging techniques. (These topics will be described in detail later in the book.)

Music for both commercials and films has to sound like a cohesive piece of music. The movie composer has the same kind of restrictions as the commercial composer, but each film cue (musical section) is generally longer than the average commercial. Some film cues can run ten or fifteen minutes, whereas very few commercials are more than one minute long.

CONCLUSION

The most important aspect of the composer's job, in both mediums, is to be able to capture the essence of the film. This is very subjective. The film composer must understand what emotions the director is trying to communicate with the music. Some directors may want scenes scored to reflect the literal action (e.g., fight scene) or obvious emotional aspect (e.g., romantic) of the film; others may have a completely different view of the emotional content the music should play.

The same criterion applies to the advertising creatives. Five directors working on a project bring five different overall points of view to the project, as do creative teams working on the same commercial. It is the composer's job to uncover the essence of what is wanted and to achieve that goal.

ASSIGNMENTS

1. Videotape a scene from a motion picture. Analyze the musical composition and its relationship to the scene. What does the music accomplish? Would the scene be just as affective without the music? Why or why not?
2. Videotape a commercial. Analyze the musical composition and its relationship to the scene. What does the music accomplish? Would the scene be just as affective without the music? Why or why not?

3

Musical Skills
(How to Approach Composition for Commercials)

Music is a unifying and liberating campaign element. It is now the 16th year of the "Best Part of Wakin' Up" campaign I helped create for Folgers Coffee. The signature music has given us flexibility and infinite variety, and it allows us to immediately own the advertising in any media.

—Arthur Meranus, former creative director of Cunningham & Walsh,
former creative director of N. W. Ayer, and former global creative director of DMB&B

Musical styles have always been associated with other creative and sociological aspects of society that occurred during a particular time period. That is the reason musical periods are usually called by the same name given to art, architecture, and other defining elements; the Classical, Baroque, and Romantic periods and the music of the 1950s and 1960s are but a few examples.

The lyrical content of songs has always reflected the times. During wars, there are patriotic songs and antiwar songs; songs about drugs define the 1960s. Dances also reflect the times, for example, swing music and the Lindy Hop define World War II and continue into the 1950s. *Saturday Night Fever* defined not only the disco era of the late 1970s but also a certain lifestyle—that of a working class family in New York. The tremendous influence of the Beatles in the 1960s was not limited to their music. The Beatles were equally influential in shaping the youth culture of the Western world. All of these musical examples are used by advertising agencies to generate ideas. In most commercials, contemporary society is the focal point of the advertising. This is reflected in the musical, cinematic, and sociological content of a commercial.

It is advantageous for the commercial composer to have a thorough knowledge of contemporary popular music as well as of traditional classical (meaning historic periods) and ethnic music of various cultures. Understanding musical history helps the composer guide the advertising agency to various styles of music that might work well for their campaign. Certain story lines might reflect a specific time period. If the composer has musical knowledge of the period, her valuable suggestions might help guide the creatives in new directions. In addition, knowing various styles makes it much easier for the composer to replicate sounds.

Listening to the radio, buying music CDs in various styles, watching films and television, attending concerts, and studying scores can help the composer become familiar with various music genres and be aware of musical trends and styles. It is important to pay attention to the timbre of the drums, bass, guitars, unique musical patterns, unusual synthesizer sounds, and other instruments. Sounds, especially in contemporary popular musical styles, become trends. For example, in dance music (club music) the 909 drum machine has produced the most popular drum sounds to achieve an authentic-sounding drum track in the house music style. In addition to sounds, certain musical patterns can define a style within a time period, which, in dance music, could mean only six months.

A pulsating repetitive synthesizer line, usually with a 16th note delay (repeated notes), is an example of a rhythmic trend that defines a genre. One example would be the dance music called *Trance*; many Trance tracks have one sung line, usually a catchy phrase that is intermittently repeated throughout the song.

In some dance music, the bass drum (kick) sound is long and deep, usually played with an 808 drum machine kick with a long delay mixed with a more defining 909 kick sound. The bass is usually coupled with a sub-bass, and the entire bass sound consists of muted-sounding definable notes that are not heard; the sound just creates a very low rhythmic thumping groove that fits with the kick drum. The sub-bass sound is used because dance clubs have sub-bass speakers; the sub-bass from the track creates an incredible low end that adds to the excitement of the music.

There are also trends in the overall sound of mixes (the final recording). Sometimes, bass and drums are emphasized; other times guitar is the most prominent instrument. The use of unusual effects, such as reverbs and special effects, also define trends. For this reason, music is referred to in time periods, for example, the "sound of the fifties," the classical period, swing, and other musical eras.

> An example of how an effect contributed to a hit record can be heard in Cher's hit "Believe," in which an unusual effect is used on her vocal. It almost made her sound as if she were yodeling. The same effect was used on many recordings after the worldwide success of that record. (This effect was created with the Antares Auto Tune computer plug-in.)
>
> Phil Spector, a very successful producer in the 1960s, developed a style that was referred to as the "Wall of Sound." It had many effects and a definitive "soundscape," combined with unique arrangement techniques that became the signature of his productions. This is an ideal example of how musical production can establish a trend. Many producers tried to emulate his sound.

The Internet is an excellent research tool, where almost any information required to tackle an assignment can be found. Stylistic recordings and the tuning parameters of unusual instruments and esoteric recordings (difficult to find in record stores) are just some of the kinds of information that can be found on the Internet.

Specialty record stores are also valuable for research. For example, some stores carry only world music, some carry only dance music, and others have only old vinyl records. These stores stock recordings that cannot be found in the average record store; the same applies to sheet music.

It is crucial to learn certain musical and technical skills. Included in these skills are:

1. How to achieve musical authenticity
2. MIDI (Musical Instrument Digital Interface)
3. Digital audio
4. Technical studio knowledge as it applies to music production (e.g., use of effects, reverbs, etc.)
5. Arranging and orchestration (covered in a separate chapter)

Modern popular composition is directly linked to this knowledge. The following is a discussion of these skills.

AUTHENTICITY

The creatives often request that the music emulate a particular time period or a specific style. One of the main problems encountered by the composer is how to achieve authenticity. It is apparent when this goal is not achieved; unfortunately, it is common to hear music that sounds contrived.

> Very often creatives play musical examples from another commercial, a movie soundtrack, a CD, or some other source. The copyright laws protect the sounds of records (or other forms of recorded music) as well as the actual notes of songs or instrumental compositions; these are called "soundalikes." If a recording is re-created, it is also considered a soundalike. If the composer decides to use a sample (recording and playing back a part of an existing recording, music, or effects), sample clearance rights must be obtained. Usually this requires paying a fee and should be handled through an attorney or a sample clearance company. There is a landmark case involving a singer that imitated Bette Midler on a music track for a Ford commercial, in which Bette Midler sued and won a very large settlement.

The author arranged a series of commercials for Burlington Coat Factory, for which the client licensed the song "Shop Around," which was originally recorded by Smokey Robinson and the Miracles. Even though the client had the rights to the song, they did not have the rights to copy the original arrangement; also, the singers could not sound like the original singers. Before the commercial was put on the air, a musicologist was hired to analyze the recordings for plagiarism. A male lead singer and a female lead singer were both recorded, and the agency opted to air the female so there could be no claim that the singer sounded like Smokey Robinson.

This being said, the composer can still replicate a sound without committing plagiarism.

It is important to be able to analyze arranging (orchestration) and compositional styles and to observe patterns and musical rules that identify a style of music within a historical time period. The following section contains specific examples of music styles.

Throughout his entire career, Johann Sebastian Bach, one of the world's great composers, copied and arranged other composers' works in order to learn their styles. This is an excellent method to help a student learn and should be periodically practiced with all styles of music. Many stylistic elements become easily recognizable when one studies music in detail; this tool makes it easier to duplicate a style. The harmonic structure, voicings, instrumentation, and musical form, along with many other elements of a musical style, can be learned through this teaching method.

In the study of Western music history, from the beginning of codified music, there were musical rules that were strictly followed. From the Gregorian chants and the music of the Renaissance, to the Baroque, Classical, Romantic, and twentieth century styles, there have always been rules of harmonization and rhythm. Certain combinations of instruments became identifiable with a musical period. For example, the basso continuo, also called thorough-bass, is a notational system developed during the Baroque period. The bass part and treble part, which made up the melody, were the only written notes. The continuo was used at a time when music was beginning to be conceived as consisting of a melody and a harmony. A harmonic code, called figured bass, was placed above or below the bass line, and the harmonies were defined through musical symbols. This part was played by a keyboard or lute and improvised by the musicians. The bass part, called the continuo, was played by a harpsichord, clavier, or lute along with a violoncello, bass gamba, or bassoon.

If the assignment is to write in the Baroque style, that does not necessarily mean to write a continuo with figured bass. The Baroque period lasted from 1600 until 1750 and contained many styles of music.

If the assignment is to write something that is in a contemporary popular style, does that mean rock, rhythm and blues, jazz, or dance? Make sure that the musical direction is well defined.

Often, the creatives listen to currently popular music in order to get musical ideas for a commercial. Around the same time that a Gregorian chant was used on a wine commercial, a group of monks from Spain recorded an album of Gregorian chants that was a popular hit. It was this album that inspired the creatives to use a Gregorian chant on their commercial.

Gregorian chant dates back to Pope Gregory I (Gregory the Great), who was Pope from 590 to 604. To achieve an authentic sound, it is important to know that Gregorian chant consisted of 1) an unaccompanied men's chorus singing in Latin (monks usually sang this music), 2) a single line melody with no harmony, 3) music that was unemotional in attitude, because the music served the religious text rather than the beauty of the singing, and 4) a scale system that was not major or minor.

Gregorian chant is written in various formats; ask the creatives which format is the most appropriate for the project you are working on. It can be sung as *antiphonal* (two choirs with alternating lines), *responsorial* (the soloist sings and the congregants respond), or *direct* (sung without alteration).

In addition to the three performance styles mentioned (antiphonal, responsorial, and direct), there were many compositional rules that governed Gregorian chant. It would be essential to study the written music (which has all been converted to modern notation) and listen to well-performed recordings to understand the rules. Listening can be especially helpful while in the recording studio, because it provides a reference point for the singers. It is also important to hire singers who perform in this style, because they will already be versed in the nuances and feel of the music.

The same general approach taken for studying Gregorian chant should be adapted to jazz, R&B (hip-hop), gospel, country, ethnic, and popular music. There are elements in all periods of music that identify their styles.

JAZZ

Jazz is America's music. It is taken from the slaves who sang music while working in the fields and started in New Orleans. The music developed into an extraordinarily complex and unique form of American music and produced some of the greatest instrumentalists and singers of any genre of music. There is no other current style of (Western) music that has its basis in improvisation. The unique harmonic jazz language, which developed from this music, has been the inspiration for most other forms of American music. This includes the music of George Gershwin, Duke Ellington, Aaron Copland, Steely Dan, B. B. King, Kenny G., and many other musicians and composers. Different styles of jazz are associated with different time periods.

> The Middle Ages was an important period in Western musical history. Although notation systems existed prior to the Middle Ages, musical notation underwent rapid development during this period, making it possible for music to be written down, so musicians other than the composer could play it. Musical rules were invented that included modes (eight musical scales) and rules of rhythm and harmony.
>
> Jazz combines improvisation and musical notation with rhythm and harmony. A jazz composition varies each time it is played, because of the improvised solos that are performed. The tune is always the same, because the underlying rhythmic and harmonic structure remains the same. The basic harmonic structure for most jazz compositions has been documented in written form, with some combination of notation and identification of harmonic structure (chord changes) along with an indication of the number of bars, the tempo, and the time signature.

A form of jazz called *Dixieland* is associated with New Orleans, and has been used on many commercials that are associated with that city. Most commercials promoting the Mardi Gras have Dixieland scores and New Orleans funeral band music, which is also unique to the region and, therefore, creates an instant identity.

> It is important to know the proper instrumentation of a particular style. For example if the assignment is to create a Dixieland piece, in addition to knowing the style, the composer should know that an authentic instrumental combination would be a cornet (not a trumpet), a clarinet or soprano saxophone, a piano, and sometimes a banjo, trombone, and drums. The size of the ensemble can vary, but the basic sound cannot.

Swing music was most popular in the late 1930s and 1940s. There have been many films depicting World War II, and the music featured was swing. Target Stores re-created the popular dance the Lindy Hop in a series of commercials that depicted the time period, but with contemporary-looking dancers. There has been a resurgence of swing music, with many swing dance clubs opening throughout the United States and Europe.

> Let us assume that the assignment is to create the sound of the Glenn Miller Band. The unique sound of that band came from many years of Miller experimenting with instrumental combinations. The final signature sound was that of a clarinet used in place of the traditional alto saxophone as the lead instrument of the saxophone section. The band also had a fluid and polished sound, which resulted from Miller's penchant for perfection; the Miller Band was never sloppy.
>
> Let us also assume that a commercial required vocals depicting the same time period. A vocal group called The Modernaires sang with the Glenn Miller Band. Their lead singer was a female backed by three men, which made their musical style and feel very distinct.

If this were the assignment, it would behoove the composer to ask the agency to hire a musicologist to determine if there could be a soundalike copyright problem. The agency might have to get permission from both the Glenn Miller estate and The Modernaires to re-create their sounds.

Tip: If the creatives ask for a re-creation of a particular vocal or instrumental group, make sure to listen to only the popular recordings; the public's perception of a "sound" comes from hearing certain recordings for a long period of time. Not all songs or instrumentals by a particular group have a consistency; therefore, if the wrong composition is chosen as an example, and the composer emulates that piece, the result may not accomplish the assignment.

The author worked on a campaign for Entenmann's cakes. One of the spots had to capture the sound of a recording that could have been made in the 1930s. In order to help achieve that, the engineer recorded the beginning of a vinyl record and looped it (repeated it) throughout the track; to re-create the ambience of a 78-rpm recording. Several popular records of the 1930s were referenced while mixing. The final product accurately depicted that time period.

It is important to note that if the same assignment were for a film, the composer would have a longer time to re-create the sound; the commercial composer must work within a shorter time frame and with a smaller budget.

ADDITIONAL TIPS

In the 1950s, 1960s, and 1970s, the Hammond B3 organ with a Leslie speaker was the organ sound heard on most records. The Hammond has a very distinct sound that is difficult to duplicate; it would behoove a composer who wanted to re-create the sound to rent a B3 with a Leslie speaker for the recording session. A typical 1950s-sounding ballad would traditionally have:

1. The piano playing triplets
2. Maybe a tenor or baritone saxophone
3. The musical chord progression: I, VI, II, V
4. Background singers singing typical traditional syllables

The purpose of the preceding examples is not to give a tutorial on specific projects, but to give examples of the kinds of things one might research to accomplish a musical goal.

THE LATIN MARKET

The Hispanic population in the United States is expected to be more than 50 percent of the total in the very near future; most major clients advertise in the Spanish language and gear their commercials to the various Hispanic cultures. Within the Spanish-speaking communities, there are many subgroups with their own, very specific, cultures. This directly affects the choice of music used in commercials.

Dr. Raul Murciano Jr. teaches at the University of Miami School of Music. He is an expert in writing music for commercials aimed at the Spanish-speaking markets. The following is a synopsis of a discussion on this subject.

In the early 1960s, there was a huge exodus of Cubans who moved to Miami, Florida, as a result of Castro and the Cuban Revolution; this exodus has continued for many years. In the past five to ten years other Spanish-speaking people from many countries have also moved to the Miami area (e.g., people from Colombia, Venezuela, Nicaragua, and other Central and South American countries), but the Cuban population still remains in the majority.

This presents a problem for the composer: how to choose the style of music that will appeal to the various cultures.

The first concern of the advertising agency is in their choice of voice-over talent. Each culture has its own idioms and pronunciations that are indicated by the announcer and/or actors. This is important for the composer to know, because it gives the best indication of the target market. Fortunately, most singers in Spanish do not have a specific accent and so they sound generic; the one exception is the accent from Spain, which has a noticeable lisp sound (most British singers also have a generic accent when singing). What *is* important is the tone of the voice. Various cultures have different styles of singing, which include the tone of voice as well as the use of melismas (decorative phrases). The composer has to be sure to hire singers who sing with the proper tone and style of the particular country or region being targeted.

The creatives will generally specify the rhythm and feel of the music they are looking for. As is the case with most Anglo commercials, more often than not, creatives want music that emulates what is currently being played on the radio stations. In the case of Hispanic commercials, the music should emulate music played on Latin radio stations. If the music is to imitate an older style, creatives will want something as close as possible to the example they provide. As mentioned previously, it is very important not to plagiarize.

Since Hispanic music varies between countries and regions within those countries, the native musicians "feel" the music in their own particular style. Even if the rhythms in different countries are basically the same, the performers' interpretations will vary. Therefore, it is important to hire musicians who will play an authentic-sounding part. (This concept will be discussed in the next section.)

If the assignment is to compose one commercial that will be played in many Spanish-speaking countries, how does one write generic music that will appeal to all of these countries? This is very difficult to accomplish. Most of the time different arrangements of the same music will be written in a particular style that appeals to one nationality. Sometimes only one music track is completed and used in many countries.

Example: Dr. Murciano was asked to write a generic composition for Visa International that would be played throughout South America. The target market was affluent people who lived an elegant lifestyle. The film did not depict a certain culture and was generic in its look—it could have been filmed in any South American country. Dr. Murciano analyzed the film and came to the conclusion that since all of these cultures shared a common European background, he would give the music a symphonic treatment, using traditional instruments, which gave the music an aristocratic feel. He mixed it with instruments such as the guitar, which are used in many South American countries, and the instruments were not played in an ethnic style that could be identified with any particular culture.

This choice of musical approach resulted from a conversation Dr. Murciano had had with the creatives on how to appeal to all cultures in their target market. Since it is very possible that the creatives might not have been aware of the potential musical problem, they were very pleased with Murciano's creative solution.

This is another example of how specific a composer has to be with the agency people. A mistake in solving this musical problem could have cost the client many millions of dollars, as a result of a lack of interest from a particular culture. When sales decline, agencies lose accounts.

Author's example: While working a series of commercials for Dr Pepper, the author had to adapt the same jingle to various Spanish and English styles. Latin house music and hip-hop were the chosen styles. The commercials had to be recorded in various lengths and sung in Spanish, mostly Spanish, mostly English, and Spanglish, which is a mixture of both languages. Not only were numerous compositional changes necessary to make each version sound complete, but also many creative questions had to be answered before writing could begin.

Again we are dealing with the importance of research. There are many forms of Spanish music from the Caribbean, Mexico, South America, as well as Spain, and they vary in musical styles and pronunciation. Therefore, it was important to find out the target audience. In this case, the client did not want the Caribbean sound (e.g., Cuban and Puerto Rican styles), because Dr Pepper has a relatively small market share in the Northeastern United States, where there is a large population of Puerto Rican and Cuban immigrants. Instead it wanted to appeal more to Mexican-Americans and the general Latino population, because Dr Pepper has a large market share in the Western United States, which has a very large Mexican-American population. None of the music was arranged in a traditional Mexican musical style, because Dr Pepper wanted to appeal to a young audience that does not listen to or identify with traditional forms of Latin music; instead Latin house music, which is dance (disco) music with Latin percussion, and hip-hop, which is a black genre, were chosen.

HIRE MUSICIANS AND SINGERS WHO ARE SKILLED IN A PARTICULAR STYLE

Studio musicians and singers are usually skilled in many styles, but some are particularly good in certain genres. It is important to learn their strengths. For example, if the assignment is to write a sonata for violin and piano in the style of the Classical Period, a violinist familiar with that style would know that certain musical ornamentation was not written down but expected to be added by the player. Most country singers and musicians use generic vocal and instrumental ornamentations that clearly characterize a style of music. [Listen to track #8 on the enclosed CD.]

The Author's Interview with Alfred Brown, a First-Call Studio Viola Player in New York City

Alfred Brown, a graduate of the Curtis Institute, produces records and is a musician's contractor for commercials, films, television, and records.

Question: "What makes a good studio musician?"

Alfred: "The best studio musicians have eclectic backgrounds. Their ability to read music is well above average . . . not only reading the notes but reading dynamics and knowing styles. You might get someone from the Philharmonic who can read the notes, but they don't necessarily have the feel of a studio musician, because a studio musician knows what goes with a particular kind of music. That can be said for all musicians—for drummers, for guitar players, for saxophone players—they have a feel—the best thing I can say about them is that they have a good sense of music like a chamber music player. They are very sensitive to each other['s playing]. You can come into a room and read the music down once, and by the second time, you've got a very good idea of what the music feels like—what it sounds like—what the nuances are, and what the leader wants.

"One of the most important things is that we have no time to rehearse, and you have to read it [the parts] almost like a performance. People like David Nadien [past concertmaster of the New York Philharmonic] can read beautiful solos in a way that sounds like a finished performance. There are severe time restrictions [because of budget], so everything has to be done as quickly as possible."

Question: "How does one train to become a studio player?"

Alfred: "The only training that I know of is by actually doing it. I think that playing chamber music is the best training. They have to feel the other players in the room—to be sensitive to the other players around them.

"When you are looking at a part, you might hear that part somewhere else in the orchestra, and you listen to the way that person plays it or that person might have heard you playing it earlier—no part in the orchestra is by itself. You always listen very carefully to what is going on around you."

Question: "Do you think that rhythm section players are categorized more than the other sections?"

Alfred: "I would say yes." [Many section players specialize in a particular style.]

Question: "How about brass players?"

Alfred: "They tend to be categorized into jazz players or classically trained players, but many of them cross over. Jazz players are not called upon to play strictly classical music, so they can cross over if they are really good."

Question: "How do classically trained players become familiar with popular styles?"

Alfred: "I think you have to listen to different kinds of music. [In the case of string players,] you have to listen to the articulation of the bowings, for instance, and how a section plays, because sections usually play together—they play pretty much the same feel. Pop phrasing is very often different than classical phrasing."

Question: "Is there any other advice you would like to offer?"

Alfred: "Be open and play chamber music as much as possible—ensemble playing."

A musicians' contractor (referred to as a "contractor") specializes in hiring the most skilled musicians for an assignment; they also submit the contracts that are required by the various unions. This is a highly specialized skill and a full-time job. If the composer needs to hire musicians who play unusual ethnic instruments, a good contractor will know where to find them. For example, the Broadway production of *The Lion King* requires numerous African instrumentalists. Not only do the musicians have to be able to play the score, but they also must come across well as actors, because the audience sees them.

LEARN HOW TO COMPOSE AND ARRANGE
IN THE GENERIC STYLE OF THE INSTRUMENTS

Many composers and arrangers write music using their own instrument of choice. One of the dangers of doing this is the limitation that can be displayed by not hearing (internalizing) the generic sound of the instruments they are trying to write for. Composers impose compositional limitations by using only their own instruments when composing music. If they have limited technical ability, the part will be limited.

> While writing for strings, it is imperative that the composer has knowledge of bowing. Bowing cannot be heard on a piano but can be internalized in the composer's mind. A legato (smooth) passage requires smooth bowing that is indicated by bow markings in the music and by an arco marking. Pizzicato is a plucking of the strings and creates a very unique effect. Tremolo is when the bow moves quickly across the strings, creating a trembling effect. Very high parts written for the violins will sound thin in the studio if there are not enough violinists playing the same part.

It is in a composer's best interest to try to internalize the part first and then write the notes. This technique should be applied to all parts that a live player would perform. "Hearing" the instrument (internalizing) will enable the composer to capture its true essence.

One should hire native musicians to perform a composition written in a typical folkloric style. The use of ethnic instruments requires a complete understanding of not only the technical limitations of the instruments but also of the creative playing style. There are typical rhythms, patterns, and ornamentations that are native to the playing of particular instruments. Even if a musician knows how to play the instrument, it will not sound authentic if the musician is not involved in the culture and customs of the native society.

> The Census Bureau asked for a group of twelve commercials that required various authentic styles, such as Arabic, Polish, and Russian. (Many examples of each musical genre were available on the Internet.) The commercials were to stress the benefits of filling out a Census report. This assignment also addressed the problem of changing musical and emotional moods within the same commercial. Each spot opened in the native country of a particular family and evolved into that same family living in the United States. Understanding the style and technical limitations of ethnic instruments helped to achieve authenticity. In this case, each composition had to change from a native style into an American jazz composition, incorporating the original theme. Because of budget restrictions, the number of musicians had to be limited. The solution was to hire three to four native musicians and six to eight contemporary musicians, and adding synthesizers helped to achieve a rich sound without destroying the feel.
>
> Tip: The commercials aimed at the Russian audience and the Polish audience both required the use of an accordion. In most cases, when thinking about an accordion, an American composer would think of the instrument that is commonly played at social gatherings. But this would have been a mistake, because there are generic Polish and Russian accordions, each with its own distinct sound. The announcers spoke the Russian and Polish languages because the commercials were directly geared toward an audience that had immigrated to the United States. The agency assigned a Russian creative for the Russian commercials and a Polish creative for the Polish spots. Both executives paid very close attention to detail, and both focused on achieving an authentic representation of their native music.
>
> The Arabic commercials presented an even more challenging assignment. Four native instruments were used: a *nay* (a flute made of cane with six finger holes and one thumb hole), an *ud* (also spelled *oud*—a short-necked, plucked guitar-like instrument), native drums, which included a *duff* (also spelled *daff*—a one-headed drum that rattles with a tambourine-type sound when struck) and a *darabukka* (a one-headed drum made of pottery, wood, or metal). In addition, the jazz ensemble included a piano, electric bass, and drums.
>
> The nay player brought nays in all keys. To make things even more difficult, one of the commercials used music composed by Mozart. The challenge was to begin the commercial with Mozart being played in an Aramaic style and transitioning into a jazz version of the same music.
>
> The arranger had to understand which compositional devices would create an Aramaic sound. Aramaic arrangements usually include the melody performed in unison or octaves. Aramaic has certain rhythmic

patterns that are popular, much the same way that Latin music produces different rhythms in, for example, the mambo, rumba, and cha-cha. After experimenting, it was decided to play the first part of the music in a traditional, ethnic, rubato, emotional style (the film dictated emotion) and then transition into an upbeat jazz groove with a faster tempo, adding contemporary instruments. The piano assumed the melody in a jazz style, and the Aramaic instruments played fills. This musical solution brought the ethnic feeling of the Arabic homeland into a new life in the United States. The music told the story of the film.

Because the campaign involved a total of twelve commercials (six for radio and six for television), there was a two-month period to experiment with the music. This is an unusually long period of time to work on a commercial. Besides creating authenticity, the most difficult part of the assignment was writing the transitions from the native-sounding part of the music to the jazz sections. Many hours were spent experimenting.

The music used for one of the Polish commercials was a very popular song in Poland. Because most of the audience would recognize the composition, the creative in charge had the composer work with the arranger prior to recording, to ensure that the musical interpretation would be accurate. Although this approach could have been uncomfortable, the composer was a very good musician and cooperative, which made for a pleasant collaboration.

Budget restrictions have been a problem throughout musical history. In fact the string quartet developed as a result of budget restrictions. The symphonies in the late 1700s and 1800s could not always be played with multiple string players on each part, therefore, each part was often restricted to one player—thus the evolution of the trio, or quartet, or sometimes a quintet. Some of the smaller churches could not afford to pay more than one player; sometimes the number of musicians was limited by choice (H. C. Robbins Landon, editor, *The Mozart Compendium*, Borders Press, 82).

It is conceivable to be asked to compose and arrange music in fifties, hip-hop, Latin, pop, and classical styles all in one week. No matter how diverse, the creatives will expect all of the tracks to sound authentic. It is surprising how many commercials do not contain music that captures the essence of the intended style.

The more varied the composer's ability to write in various genres, the better her chance of receiving numerous assignments.

Some Common Mistakes Composers and Arrangers Make When Writing for Unfamiliar Instruments

Many composers and arrangers write for instruments they are unfamiliar with. When this happens, the sound will certainly not be authentic, and the part will sound contrived. In writing music for commercials and film, ethnic instruments are sometimes used to achieve a unique feeling or ambience. It is important to become familiar with the native sounds, nuances (playing style), and technical and musical limitations of an instrument before writing a part for it. [Listen to tracks #2–6 on the enclosed CD.]

Ethnomusicology is the study of music of non-Western cultures. George Harrison, of the Beatles, did more to promote the synthesis of ethnic instruments in traditional pop music than any other musician. He studied the sitar (a guitar-like Indian instrument) with the world-renowned Indian classical sitar player Ravi Shankar. He then proceeded to use the sitar on the Beatles albums *Rubber Soul, Sgt. Pepper's Lonely Hearts Club Band,* and several others. This was the beginning of what is now known as World Music. *Billboard,* the leading music magazine, has a contemporary World Music chart that is printed every week.

Ethnic instruments (which are unusual in other societies) are played and tuned in a particular manner. Instruments that have the same name (e.g., balaphone, an African xylophone) may have different tunings in different countries.

Most ancient instruments have limitations. For example, most wooden flute players have many flutes, each tuned in a different key.

The typical playing style of the *kora* (an African lute harp) incorporates the use of triplets. The kora player has to change tuning (in a manner similar to tuning a guitar) when playing in various keys. The kora is not a chromatic instrument.

Author's experience: The kora has twenty-one strings made of fishing line. It can only be played in certain keys and is tuned to those various keys by moving bundles of line wrapped around its neck. We used this instrument in a commercial that required an African feel. Because of the instrument's unique structure, it's important to know its limitations before writing any music for it. Like many other instruments, the kora is traditionally played in a very distinct style. Because of this, the composer should listen to recordings to learn as much as possible about the generic sound and style of the instrument. It would be advisable for the composer to consult with the instrumentalist to find out if the part can be played and if the traditional style can be adapted to it. If it is not written properly, the part could sound awkward.

Writing for ethnic instruments requires research and study in order to compose and produce authentic-sounding music. However, it is just as important for a composer to be familiar with the more common genres like R & B, rock, new age, jazz, and pop.

Example: A harp is not a chromatic instrument. If the composer does not know how much time it takes for the player to manipulate the pedals, the written part could be impossible to perform. One suggestion is to call the musician and ask questions. It is improbable that an orchestrator/arranger will know the nuances of every instrument. Knowing the best pitch range (tessitura) of each instrument is essential.

The following are some examples of common problems that composers encounter:

Writing in the wrong register. A part might sound good on a piano or synthesizer but might not sound good when it is played on the real instrument.

Some synthesizers are able to sound past the actual register of the real instrument they are trying to emulate. For your music to sound authentic, you must pay attention to this potential problem and know the range of the instruments you're writing for and their best-sounding registers.

Not using the proper voicings or harmonies when composing or arranging in a particular style. Example: If writing in the classical style, there must be an understanding of the harmonic and compositional rules of that time. The same holds true when writing music for the Baroque and all other musical time periods. In contemporary popular music there is extensive use of samples (digital recordings that can be played back with a keyboard) and electronic music. Know the nuances of the style.

Not checking the key with a singer before choosing a key. The key affects the emotional feeling of a composition. If the key is too high, the voice can sound strained; if it is too low, it can sound lackluster; the key might be physically out of range for a particular singer. The safest strategy is to audition the key with the singer before finalizing the arrangement.

Not realizing that the key of the composition directly affects the mood of the music. Playing a composition in various keys brings a completely different feeling and mood to the same composition. A high key can sound lively, whereas a lower key can sound too dark.

Using inappropriate instruments for a particular style. If a composer/arranger were trying to emulate music written in 1948, use of an electric bass guitar would not be appropriate, because the instrument was not invented until 1951. If the assignment were to write in a traditional symphonic form, the saxophone would probably not be used, except for some special effect. Don't let music get in the way of dialogue. If they're in the same frequency range, the scene will sound too busy. [Listen to track #9 on the enclosed CD.]

The foregoing are some of the pitfalls that can be experienced if careful attention is not given to all composing and arranging decisions.

MIDI

MIDI is the acronym for musical instrument digital interface. Synthesizers are made by many different manufacturers, and plugging them into a MIDI enables them to synchronize with each other and play back simultaneously. Most synthesizers enable the use of sixteen MIDI tracks per device, which means that sixteen individual events (channels or sounds) per synthesizer and its associated MIDI-based hardware, such as reverb unitsm can be triggered on an individual basis. MIDI provides digital data, not sounds; the individual synthesizers produce the sounds.

Computers have changed the world in much the same way as satellites, radio, television, telephones, films, and every other form of communication have. The ability to use MIDI is one of the most important technical skills a composer/arranger in any musical idiom can have. It has revolutionized the way music is written and performed. To the composer of commercials, the technical applications are just as important as the music.

SEQUENCERS

Sequencers enable a composer to arrange a composition one track at a time and to play back MIDI and audio data, simultaneously triggering various synthesizers, which produce the sounds. Sequencers provide a recording platform, nonlinear editing, and performance playback: events such as sustain, velocity, aftertouch (the pressure applied to a note after the initial attack affects the output level), pitch bends, transposition, and other parameters. Most sequencers provide detailed editing systems, enabling the programmer to accomplish almost any imaginable sound manipulation.

Most sequencers are computer programs, although there are stand-alone hardware sequencers, which are less popular. Computer-based sequencers can be connected to video players, making it possible to play the music in synchronization with the video. Most computer sequencers look like tape recorders, with virtual playback, record, fast forward, and rewind buttons. Many sequencers have a window that displays the actual musical notation that has been played into the system; this notation can be edited and printed. (Programs such as Finale are dedicated notation programs and are more advanced than those found in a sequencer program. Many professional copyists use this type of program.)

In any genre of film writing, the composer has to time the scenes and decide on the tempo or tempos before composing music. Since the music has to match the action (both emotional and physical) in most cases, it is very difficult to conduct live musicians without the aid of some form of metronome; it is also difficult to play back electronic music in time with the action, without a form of synchronization. Once a tempo or tempos have been chosen, the sequencer provides essential technical information instantaneously, which enables the programs to play in sync.

> When a sequencer is connected to a video player, the composer can roll the tape to a particular scene, and the computer will display bar numbers, and real time and SMPTE frame numbers (a time code), which gives an address for the specific location. For example, if the tempo were 120 beats per minute, the indicator might read that the action takes place on the third beat of bar fifteen. The composer compiles a list of markers, describing the action, which then serves as a guide to composing the final composition. Next to the markers is the SMPTE number, bar number, tempo, and real time. (These will be discussed in detail in the chapter devoted to compositional techniques.)

One of the key changes that electronic music has provided is enabling the composer/arranger to program music that would be impossible for a live musician to play. The most obvious example is the programming of drums, using very complex rhythms with numerous percussion instruments being played simultaneously. Special effects (delays, various reverbs, etc.) are added to the mix, which gives the final drum part a unique sound that could not be achieved through traditional methods. The same theory can apply to other parts. Because of this freedom, the composer has to take this technology into account when producing music. Because of the technology, virtually any musical thoughts that are in the composer's mind can be expressed in some musical form. This is the primary difference between composing for traditional instruments played by live musicians and using electronic instruments alone or in combination with live players.

Another feature of most sequencers is the automated recording and mixing system. There is a graphic display of a recording console, which works in the same manner as a real tape recorder and recording console. The transport controls show a record button, fast forward and rewind buttons, and a stop button. As previously mentioned, the bar numbers and beats are displayed in a separate window, which enables the programmer to also read real time and SMPTE time codes. The mixing console shows faders with send buttons, pan buttons, and automation buttons and voice and track assignment buttons. The individual faders can adjust the level. The aux send buttons enable the use of effects like reverb, EQ (equalization), which can alter the frequencies (treble, mid-range, bass, etc.), and other parameters that are included within a hardware version of a recording console. After the music has been programmed, all of the individual sounds (tracks) have to be mixed together, forming a final musical combination called a mix.

DIGITAL AUDIO

Digital audio has revolutionized recording. With digital audio, the analog sound is converted into a binary code composed of 0s and 1s and then reconverted to analog through the use of digital to audio converters (D to A converters) so the sound can be heard through a speaker system. Digital sound cannot be heard without this conversion. There is an ongoing debate as to how pleasing the sound of digital is. Some people like the sound because it is pristine—very clean and clear. Others would rather have what they consider the "warmer" sound of analog tape. Most rock and roll bands prefer analog, because they feel it has a "dirtier" sound and a deeper bottom end; most pop and R & B music is recorded in a digital format, because producers like the crisp, clear sound. It is a matter of personal choice. Both formats are used in all styles of music.

A third option is called Dolby SR (spectral recording), which is a noise-reduction system used with analog tape that improves noise reduction up to 24bd over systems without it. The result is a quiet and warm sound. Many producers prefer the Dolby SR format to plain analog or digital recording because of the warmer sound.

The following are some of the advantages to digital audio:

The principal advantage of digital technology is the ability to copy and combine information without a loss of quality. With analog recording (the traditional recording method), the frequency with which tracks are copied and recopied determines the amount of hiss and distortion that can be heard. With digital technology, digital numbers are stored and then converted into analog sounds to be heard. Therefore, there is no loss of quality when copying data.

The ability to perform nonlinear, nondestructive editing on software-based computer systems. Nonlinear editing enables the programmer to instantly locate any place in the program without having to fast forward to the location, as is required with a traditional tape recorder. Since there is no tape involved, the parameters of the edit are entered into the computer program, and the edit is performed immediately. Most programs work by highlighting specific regions for editing. For example, if we wanted to edit out bars 4 through 27, the programmer would highlight the region from bar 4 to bar 27 and push delete. Digital technology also allows for instantaneous multiple mixes and multiple edits. It enables the composer to experiment without a loss of quality.

Since most computer sequencing programs contain digital audio (e.g., Pro Tools, Digital Performer), basic effects plug-ins are included with most programs. Plug-ins are computer-based digital effects and signal processing units that perform the same functions as their hardware counterparts. Effects that are included in most programs are reverbs, echoes, equalizers, gates, and compressors.

As with hardware units, there are many variations and choices of plug-ins. They all sound different and offer different features. Since purchasing third-party effects can be costly, it is advisable to listen to the demo CDs provided by most manufacturers before acquiring them. Many manufacturers also offer test downloads from their websites.

Digital tape recorders (hardware versions) use digital tape. Computer-based recording programs and hard disc recording (no tape) have surpassed the use of most forms of digital tape, but there are modular digital tape systems that are still popular. Each module contains eight tracks and can be locked to several other modules, which results in a multitude of tracks that play in sync. When there are multiple units, a central controller triggers all of the machines simultaneously, enabling both recording and playback. Some programmers store their digital programs on a modular digital system and run it in tandem with the computer digital system. The most popular modular recorders are ADATS and DA 88s.

There are hardware-based digital recorders that do not require tape. Much the same as computer-based recorders, these units have nondestructive editing features.

The majority of modern recording is digital, and as the sound of digital develops, it will become even more popular. The clear sound is appealing to most music producers. To the composer/arranger, the advantages of computer-based digital technology, unquestionably, have no competition. In the near future, very little tape (analog or digital) will be used.

One of the problems with computer-based digital audio is that it requires a great deal of hard disk memory for storage and processing power to run the program. Digital plug-ins require a great deal of processing power. Running out of processing power can be frustrating and hinder the programmer from completing his creative vision. Here is some advice:

1. Buy the fastest computer and the most RAM within your budget.
2. Always save digital audio on a separate hard drive. Do not save audio on the same hard drive that contains the computer's operating system. Many problems can occur because of this practice.
3. Always burn a CD or DVD of your program as a safety measure and for future reference. Memory is a valuable commodity and even very large storage drives will eventually fill up.

SAMPLERS

A sampler can record any audio signal, convert it into digital audio (and store it in RAM), and play back through the use of MIDI. A note generated from a keyboard controller can trigger the sampled sound. There are many sampling CDs and CD ROMs for sale, containing virtually any sounds a composer could want—orchestral instruments, drum loops (grooves), sound effects, and so on.

There are two kinds of samplers: hardware-based and computer-based. The sounds can be edited, which helps to achieve a wide variety of sound manipulation. Filters, velocity, time compression (changing tempo without changing the pitch of the instrument), and the ability to truncate (erase the unwanted parts), transpose, or normalize (achieve the strongest volume level) a sound are some of the changeable parameters.

An advantage of hardware samplers is that they do not deplete the CPU (central processing unit) power, which contains the brains of the computer. When using plug-ins (effects and signal processing) with digital audio, many computers run out of memory. Using a hardware-based sampler provides many of the features of computer audio. A sampler combined with digital audio in a computer-based system is a very powerful tool for the composer.

STUDIO TECHNOLOGY AS IT APPLIES TO MUSIC PRODUCTION

Even though it is not the intention of this book to concentrate on the technical aspects of recording, there is some basic knowledge that a composer must have. The use of recording technology affects not only the overall "sound" of the final recording but also how the composer conceives of the music. For instance, a vocal might have to emulate the ambience of a church or cathedral, as did the Gregorian chant sung on a wine commercial referred to earlier; a guitar sound can be embellished with numerous delays, echoes, and other effects; for example, often guitars in surfing music have an identifiable delay.

The form that a composition or arrangement (written to be recorded) takes is directly related to the effects used on voices and instruments. There must be enough space between the notes for effects to be heard—composers or arrangers should take this into consideration when writing. Not having a thorough understanding of technology can result in a "mess of sound." Delays and echoes tend to create a cloudy soundscape, and the final music tends to have no definition of sound. The creative use of technology requires experimentation.

Whereas in the past, a composer studied traditional composition and orchestration, today that is not enough. The modern composer/arranger must also have technical knowledge in order to survive in all forms of commercial music.

An understanding of *signal processors*, *audio effects*, and the *recording console* is of utmost importance.

Signal Processors and Audio Effects

Audio effects are added to the original signal; *signal processors* change signals. The use of signal processors and audio effects has become as important in audio as it has been in film effects processing; signal processors can change a sound in infinite ways, helping the composer achieve unique sounds. The creative use of these devices is up to the composer/arranger and, in some cases, the music producer.

> For the purposes of this discussion, the terms *audio effects* and *signal processors* will be used interchangeably.

The most commonly used processors are called DSPs, which is an abbreviation for digital signal processors. Analog signals are transformed into digital signals. Analog to digital converters (A to D converters) convert the signal into the digital domain, and digital to analog converters (D to A converters) convert the signal back to the analog domain, so the sound can be heard through speakers.

The same effects that can be programmed into hardware-based processors can now be found in digital software versions. The software-based virtual processors (that are copied from hardware versions of the same processors) usually look and work almost exactly the same as the hardware version; the parameters can be adjusted with the mouse, and the computer can store the final settings. This is an important feature because it saves a substantial amount of time by being able to recall exact settings. If a session required ten hardware signal processors and each time revisions had to be made to a mix, all ten devices would have to be reset by hand. With computers, the settings can be stored and recalled.

> An advantage of a virtual signal processor is being able to automate the parameters. If the programmer wanted to increase or decrease the amount of reverb in each measure, the computer automation would remember the moves. The same goes for most plug-ins.
>
> Some hardware consoles have automated processors, but these are costly, whereas almost all software sequencer programs contain this feature.

Computer-based sequencers, which contain digital audio as well as MIDI, all include a basic set of digital processors called plug-ins. There are many third-party manufacturers making plug-ins, but not all plug-ins work with all software. Find out which manufacturers support software that will work with a particular program. Most sequencer manufacturers include a list of supported third-party vendors. This information can also be found on the manufacturers' websites.

One of the major problems encountered with the use of plug-ins is that the computer might run out of memory and not be able to support as many devices as are desired for a particular track; plug-ins are memory intensive. The program might crash or inform the user that the computer is out of memory, or it might slow down the response time to each command, becoming a hindrance to a creative environment. There are two basic solutions to this problem:

1. Add additional RAM to the computer, which creates more memory.
2. Copy an audio track, including the signal processing, to another audio track. For example, a vocal might have a delay added to it. The vocal, along with the delay, can be bounced together onto a new track, and the delay effect can then be removed from the program, thereby lessening the memory load on the CPU of the computer. This frees up memory so that another effect can be used on another part and these bounced together as in the previous example, and so on.

It is conceivable that the final mix will have six or eight tracks all containing prerecorded processing; the engineer then balances these tracks to achieve a final mixed track. One of the problems with this process is that when the tracks are balanced and a particular effect does not sound appropriate, the only solution is to rerecord that track and adjust the effect, which can be time consuming. The solutions to these problems really depend on budget, but with some creative thinking, most technical problems can be solved. The following are some commonly used processors:

Equalization (EQ). Equalizing is the ability to change sound frequencies. Every recording console, whether real or virtual, offers the composer the opportunity to alter the sound of the signal flowing through an individual fader. *EQ* (the common term) can change the sound minimally or radically. For example, adding higher frequencies can achieve clarity to a muffled-sounding vocal, and adding low frequencies can make a bass sound deeper. The engineer is able to choose the frequencies to be adjusted and add or subtract the amount in various degrees. Basic consoles will generally specify the low, midrange, and high frequency knobs; the more sophisticated the recording console, the more complex the EQ system and the better the quality of EQ.

In addition to console equalization, there are separate hardware units that can be patched into the board (console). The two most popular kinds are *parametric EQ* and *graphic EQ*.

Parametric equalizer. In this type of equalizer, the frequencies are all adjustable rather than having predetermined steps called discrete steps that are changed by clicking a knob. The knobs on parametric EQs turn smoothly while adjusting the parameters and the level of the frequency. Parametric equalizers are found on most modern consoles.

Graphic equalizer. In the graphic equalizer, the frequencies are arranged according to musical octaves. Instead of knobs, there are sliders. Frequencies are adjusted by moving the sliders in a linear fashion.

Equalization is an important part of the creative process and requires experimentation. Only the basics have been covered here.

Reverberation units. Reverb creates a feeling of space and ambience; the delays (a series of repeated echoes) are measured in milliseconds and can be adjusted. Some reverb units allow complex programming, which helps to achieve interesting effects. The size and surface material of a room can be programmed. Standard settings are: small room, large room, auditorium, cathedral, drum rooms, live-sounding rooms, and dead rooms (very minor reverb). Hundreds of combinations are offered and can be programmed with the more sophisticated units. Some reverbs have presets only. It is common to use several reverbs to achieve a desired ambience.

The software DSP (digital signal processor) versions work in the same manner. The sound and programmability vary with the manufacturer. One manufacturer may have many delay units, all with different sounds and editing parameters, while others have fewer choices. Choice of reverb units becomes a matter of individual preference. Some units are very warm sounding, while others are more resonant.

The one difference between hardware and software reverbs is that on computers some reverbs respond in real time and the changes are heard while the program is playing. In units that do not respond in real time, once a setting is chosen, the computer must process the settings before the effect can be heard. Each time a parameter is adjusted, there is a waiting period while the computer processes the change. If possible, it is much better to use real-time devices.

Delays. Delays are used to create various effects, the most common of which is to add a feeling of space and depth to a vocal or instrument. If one listens closely, on most contemporary recordings, a very faint repeating effect can be heard behind the vocals. The length of the delay (e.g., an eighth note, a sixteenth note, a dotted eighth note, or a triplet delay) depends on the desired effect. The level of the delay can be adjusted, and proper use of delays adds depth to the mix.

Another use of delays (as described earlier with the Trance music example) is to create a rhythmic, repeated effect on an instrument that actually creates a groove. An eighth note or sixteenth note delay is usually used. The most obvious question would be, Why not just write two eighth notes or four sixteenth notes for each note rather than using a delay effect? The answer is that delay units can be programmed to use additional parameters in combination with the delay (e.g., feedback, or repeats). Delays help to create a certain ambience that cannot be accomplished by just repeating notes.

> A bass part incorporating delays and feedback as part of its basic sound has to be composed with the delay in mind; the composer would almost certainly write a different part if the effect were not an intrinsic part of the basic sound. This is a perfect example of how an effect is directly related to the composition.

As mentioned previously, delay units are programmed in milliseconds. There is a formula that determines the number of milliseconds (at a determined bpm [beats per minute]) that will create the chosen delay. The formula is: $1{,}000/(bpm/60)$ = quarter-note delay in milliseconds. There is also a printed list that supplies this information at various tempos. Sometimes, just experimenting with various delays will produce the desired effect.

Another common usage is to create a doubling effect. When jingles are recorded, the backgrounds are usually doubled. This means that the singers record each part two or three times, creating a richer sound. Choosing the proper delay can almost accomplish the same effect. The difference is that when real people double the parts, the double always sounds a little different from the first part—the intonation and vibrato vary, which makes the doubled effect sound more human than the perfectly processed double. It becomes both a creative and financial decision whether to double—session fees and residual payments are higher when the performers double parts.

> Make sure that the expense of doubling is included in the budget and that the agency knows, before the session, that you plan to double. This can become expensive and will be deducted from the creative fee if it is not planned beforehand.

Delays, like EQ, can be used in creative ways. It is up to the imagination.

Compressors. Compressors will automatically attenuate a signal that goes above a programmed level called a *threshold*. It is essentially the same as lowering a fader if distortion is heard.

Compressors are commonly used in commercials. By averaging the level between the loudest and softest sections, the overall track becomes louder. In the case of rhythmic arrangements, much more power and excitement result. When used with vocals, instead of the singer sounding too loud, both the music track and the singer sound loud.

Compressors are commonly used on individual tracks for the recording of kick drums, snare drums, bass, and anything else where the dynamic range should not vary too much and the desired result is for the track to be heard in the mix without covering up other parts. If dynamics are wanted, compression should not be used; it definitely changes the sound.

A song heard on the radio sounds noticeably different from when it is heard on a CD player, because most broadcast stations have *limiters* (compressors with a higher threshold) that attenuate anything that goes above a designated threshold. This, especially with rhythmic tracks, adds energy. When the dynamics of a track are compressed, everything sounds like it's around the same level, which adds energy. Many commercials (as well as records) have special radio mixes. For example, most commercials are EQd brighter (exaggerating the higher frequencies) than an average record; the higher frequencies are attenuated on the radio, and the extra highs compensate for the loss.

Expanders increase or decrease a chosen frequency. **Noise gates** are used to mute unwanted material such as noise between recorded information. Time compression changes the tempo of a track without changing the key. (Speeding up a tape raises the key, and slowing it down makes the key lower.) **Pitch correctors** can correct poor intonation, and the **transposition** parameter can change the key. (The ability to **transpose** is usually found in computer-based sequencing program and hardware samplers.)

If a singer arrives at a session and the key is wrong, using the transposition parameter that is found in most software sequencers and samplers (hardware or software) can instantly change the key. The parameters, in sequencers, are adjusted by intervals, e.g., up one whole step, or from the key of C to the key of D. One of the problems with changing a key is that the transposition might sound unnatural—a vocal could sound like Mickey Mouse if the transposition is too radical. In addition, a change of key might require changing the octaves in which some of the instruments are played. For example, a change of key might cause the bass part to sound too high, so it would have to be lowered by one octave.

Filters. Filters are used to eliminate or reduce sections of an audio signal. For example, a hi-pass filter only allows frequencies above the designated threshold (which is adjustable) to pass, while the frequencies below are attenuated. Conversely, a low-pass filter only allows the frequencies below the threshold to be heard, and the frequencies above are attenuated. Notch filters attenuate specific frequencies. Filters can be used creatively to help achieve unusual sounds and can also be used to eliminate unwanted frequencies, such as a low hum.

Only the basics of signal processing have been covered here. There are numerous devices that create unusual results. Choices have to be made when buying gear, or the cost will be prohibitive. If there is a low budget, buy the traditional software plug-ins or hardware or a combination of both. Equalizers, reverberation units, echo units, compressors, expanders, gates, delays, and choruses are essential to recorded sound production.

THE RECORDING CONSOLE

There is a difference between a recording console and a mixing console. Recording consoles can assign channels to tape recorders or digital audio devices so the material can be recorded; mixers cannot. Other than this, they can perform the same functions. Recording consoles and mixing consoles come in both virtual (computer-based software) and hardware versions. Most composers use a combination of the two. Some consoles are analog, some are digital, and some are a combination of the two. Digital consoles currently dominate the market and will continue to do so as technology advances.

Digital recording consoles work with a computer and an interface; they convert the analog signals into digital signals and route the signals digitally. This enables the engineer to instantly recall the entire signal path because it has been stored in the computer. The most minute changes can be accomplished and recalled as many times as desired without compromising the quality of the signal; there is no loss of quality because it is digital. This process saves a lot of time and money. The digital signal path also can sound cleaner (have less distortion) than an analog signal path.

Some **analog consoles** are controlled digitally. This means that the signal path is analog but all other parameters are controlled digitally as described for the digital console. In a traditional analog console, the signal path stays in the analog domain. Each time a mix has to be recalled, all of the parameters (EQ, the patch bay configuration [a way to assign devices], the signal processing devices, etc.) have to be set by hand, but then the automation will recall the level changes.

Because audio technology has been moving at such a rapid pace, there are many affordable digital consoles on the market. Purists, who do not like the sound of digital, will use the traditional analog consoles, but the majority of recording will continue to be in the digital domain.

Sometimes an instrument or voice might sound fine when soloed, but must be adjusted when one listens to the full mix. The recording or mixing console enables the engineer to EQ (equalize) the sound of each track by adjusting the frequencies; this enables the engineer to blend the instruments more effectively.

Faders control the volume levels of each track. As previously discussed, in order to attain the best balance, levels have to be adjusted (along with the signal processing)—faders are used to perform this function. Some consoles are automated, while others must be adjusted manually. The automated faders play back the level changes. Some automation also saves and plays back the signal processing. The number of faders available depends on the console being used.

The individual faders (with signal processing) can be grouped together and bussed (sent) to **group faders**, for example, all of the drums (snare, kick, hi-hat, toms, cymbals, etc.) could be bussed to two group faders; the electric and acoustic pianos could be sent to two group faders, and so on. The level of the group faders can then be adjusted to achieve the best balance. For example, to make the drums louder the programmer or engineer only has to increase the level on two group faders rather than on the individual faders of each drum or cymbal. The balance on the combined tracks can be adjusted by changing the parameters on the individual faders, which in turn affects the overall balance on the grouped tracks. The individual faders are automated, and automation of both level and signal processing can be adjusted throughout the track.

The master fader is used to adjust the overall output level of the console. The signals from the individual faders are bussed to the master fader. If the levels from the individual faders are too hot (loud), distortion occurs. The distortion might not register on the master fader meter. All of the faders might register acceptable levels, but the overall master fader level *still* might register too "hot," resulting in a mix that sounds distorted. Listen very closely to the mix, because distortion is sometimes difficult to detect.

Pushing the **solo button**, which is located near each fader, will allow the individual track to be soloed. Soloing is useful when there are many tracks and someone wants to hear the one track quickly without having to turn down every fader.

Depressing **the mute button**, also located near each fader, will mute the individual track. This function can be programmed with the use of automation. Muting is helpful for mixing and tracking and can be a quick method for experimenting with various combinations of tracks.

Panning is the placement of sound in the audio spectrum—left, right, center, and so on. A panning potentiometer (pot) is located near the fader button. For example, the hi-hat might be panned to the right, the toms to the left, and the kick drum to the middle. Panning helps to create a soundscape. If too many instruments are panned to the same location, there will be no feeling of separation and the track will begin to sound muddy and cluttered. Panning creates a stereo environment.

Auxiliary sends bus the output signal of a track to another source; the main use is for signal processing. As the send knob is turned up, more effect is added to the signal. Aux sends are also used for monitor mixes or headphone mixes. Singers or instrumentalists usually ask to hear certain balances in their headphones, for example, a louder bass, less drums, and so on.

The engineer and music producers determine the use of the aux sends; many devices and uses can be assigned. Most consoles have eight or more aux sends.

Returns send back the processed signal to the console so it can be heard.

There are **master aux sends** and **master returns**, which provide the overall master output and input levels of the devices (reverbs, delays, etc.); they bus their signals to the individual aux sends, which are located above each fader. Each aux send can be individually adjusted to accommodate the requirements of each track.

If the master send level or return level of a reverb unit is too hot, the reverb (which is then used only on the tracks the engineer chooses) will sound distorted. This can be adjusted by lowering the input and/or output level of the device. If the master output level is too low and an individual aux send is turned up, there might be very little effect heard. The solution is to increase the level of the master send (to the aux sends) and/or master return.

Limiters, expanders, noise gates, and compressors (previously described) are built into the more expensive consoles. All of these devices are included with most digital audio programs. If these devices are not built into the console, they are used as outboard gear. They are essential to recording and mixing.

The trim knob enables the engineer to achieve additional gain to the incoming signal. For example, many instruments or microphones have a low output level, and the trim helps to increase the signal to an acceptable level.

When one is trying to balance the levels of an individual fader, frequently a signal is too low. The fader might be set as high as it will go but the output level is still too low. The trim knob will increase the level of the signal. (This is only one way of accomplishing this balance. Compressors and expanders or other solutions might also be used.)

The channel input sections enable the signal to enter the signal path, and the **channel output** enables the signal to be heard.

The assignment buttons (which are located with each fader on a recording console) assign the fader's signal to an outside source, for example, tape, hard disk, DAT (digital audio tape), and so on.

If the kick drum is on fader number one and the bass is on fader number two, the assignment button for fader number one would be pushed to number one and the assignment button for fader number would be pushed to number two (or any other output number). On many consoles there is a knob that must be turned to the left to enable odd numbers and to the right to enable even numbers. On most consoles, these buttons assign the tracks to group faders, which route the signals to the desired output source.

The monitor section routes the combined audio signals to the speakers. Some consoles have a separate monitor system that can be used for various purposes, such as for a separate headphone mix. The B monitor enables the engineer to adjust the balance without disrupting the overall balance of the A monitor.

Each fader (on most consoles) has a meter. A meter displays signal strength and distortion. As previously mentioned, some distorted signals are very subtle, and the meter reading will help determine where the distortion is coming from. The **master fader meter** reads the overall output signal from the console.

In addition to the meters, there are **clipping lights**, which are located on most fader strips. When the clipping light is lit, there is normally distortion. Most computer-based consoles also have clipping lights.

Amplifiers, preamplifiers (preamps), and phantom power are included in most consoles. **Amplifiers** boost the gain of the overall audio signal so that the speakers can attain their maximum effectiveness. Preamps boost the signal of low-level individual input signals so they can attain their maximum power; preamps also help to avoid distortion. Condenser microphones have a very low level output; the power for the microphone is provided directly from the console with phantom power. There is a button located on each fader strip that will enable that fader to use the phantom power.

All professional and many project studios have a **patch bay**. A patch bay contains all inputs and outputs from the devices in the studio setup, for example, synthesizers, reverbs, digital delays, compressor/limiters, and so on. Instead of coming out of the output of a synthesizer going to the input of a reverb unit and coming out of the reverb into the recording console, all of these functions can be activated by plugging in patches in the patch bay.

Automation is the process of adjusting console parameters (such as level, panning, signal processing, etc.) and being able to play back and continually update the changes until a satisfactory mix has been achieved. Not all consoles have automation; almost all digital audio programs have automation. Automation is the most essential element in the process of mixing, because it enables the minutest detail to be adjusted and recalled.

What have just been described are the technical basics of the recording console; the way it is used is strictly a creative process. A competent recording engineer is as essential to the recording process as any musician. The ambience of the track can sometimes mean the difference between success and failure. A good analogy is the contribution a film editor makes to a film. Creative audio editing and signal processing can also mean success or failure.

TIME CODE

In order to synchronize video and music playback, there must be a time code that enables that process to work. A time code is an address. The various signals are told to go there and work simultaneously.

The time code is made up of hours, minutes, seconds, and frames. For example, a code might read: 05 10 18 27, which means the video address is: 5 hours, 10 minutes, 18 seconds, and 27 frames. Let us assume that a car crashed at this video address. Depending on the tempo, the composer would be able to determine the measure and beat in which that event occurred. The time code is based on a twenty-four-hour cycle.

NTSC (National Television Standards Committee) is the American standard for video. There are 30 frames per second for black-and-white video; this is called non-drop frame code. Color video runs at 29.97 frames per second; this is called drop-frame time code, which means that frames are automatically dropped to make up the difference in time. With drop-frame code, there are 108 frames per hour extra, which translates to 3.6 additional seconds per hour. When using drop-frame code, 2 frames are dropped at the beginning of each minute, with the exception of every tenth minute. This corrects the timing problem.

The composer must tell the editor which tape format (VHS, etc.) and time code are being used. (Most commercials are in color and therefore require drop-frame code.) The sequencer must be set to the proper setting of either 30 frames per second or 29.97 frames per second. If the setting is wrong, synchronization will be off.

The European equivalent of NTSC is called PAL/SECAM and runs at 25 frames per second; in this format black and white and color are the same and both use non-drop frame time code. Film runs at 24 frames per second.

Time code is also used to lock several tape machines together so that they are always at the same address, enabling the music to play back in sync.

SMPTE Time Code

SMPTE (Society of Motion Picture and Television Engineers) time code (also called longitudinal time code) is the preferred code for audio and video production. Most composers have some form of videotape machine (VCR, U-MATIC, etc.). The editor will record SMPTE code on one track and dialogue on the other track. The time code is displayed on the screen (hours, minutes, seconds, and frames) and is burned in, meaning that the code has actually been added to the video and is always on the screen.

Another form of time code is VITC (Vertical Interval Time Code). In this process, the code is recorded on an address track. The advantage of using an address track is that it does not eliminate one of the two stereo audio tracks. This method requires a very expensive professional video player that is not something most composers would own. The visual time code is not necessarily burned in; it can be viewed when necessary and then hidden.

Another method of locking up with the computer sequencer is to load the picture into the computer with the use of a video capture card. This method is becoming very popular because there is no rewinding of a tape machine necessary. For example, if bar four, beat one, is the desired location, the picture and the audio can be synchronized with a push of a button on the keyboard. This is a nonlinear method and therefore saves much time.

Arranging concepts will be discussed in a later chapter.

ASSIGNMENTS

1. Play examples of studio technology as it applies to music production, that is, bring in song samples or commercials in which technology plays a large part in the sound of the recording.
2. Play an example of either an old style or an ethnic style of music that was recently created but sounds authentic. List the reasons why.

4

Analyzing Commercials
(From a Musical Point of View)

The first step in the process of developing a musical approach to a commercial is to analyze the storyboard. The storyboard outlines the commercial frame by frame through the use of drawings, dialogue, and camera instructions. All pertinent information, which includes the product name, title, and length of the commercial, is notated.

> Sometimes, it is difficult to envision what the actual film will look like, because it is hard to show movement in sketches. To be safe, have the creatives explain each frame.

A storyboard helps the creative team and business team visualize the look of the final film. As previously discussed, storyboards are usually tested in focus groups, after which revisions are normally made. The final storyboard becomes the shooting guide for the director. (In some instances, the composer is presented with the final film. This is infrequent because the music is usually a part of the initial creative process. The composer is normally involved before the storyboard is presented to the client.)

The most difficult aspect of analyzing a storyboard is the ability to understand the essence of the commercial. Since the dialogue has not been recorded and the pictures are merely sketches, it is sometimes difficult to understand the intention of the writer, which is important because it affects the attitude of the music. It is advisable to have the writer read and record the dialogue and announcer's copy prior to composing the music. Make certain the designated timing (i.e., :15, :30) is not exceeded. If the copy does not fit in the proper time frame, suggest that it be revised before approaching the composition. It will be impossible to structure the music properly without accurate timings. Listen to the dialogue while composing; it will help to achieve the proper musical mood.

Sometimes, it is not possible to have the copy recorded. In that case, it is essential that every aspect of the writer's intention be clearly explained to the composer. Since the commercial has not yet been filmed, the composer has to determine the timings frame by frame. The best approach is with a stopwatch. Read each frame or each section and note the timings on the storyboard and record it onto a DAT or CD; cassettes do not run at the proper speed and timings recorded on them will not be accurate. Make certain to leave space for action that has no dialogue. If working with a digital audio sequencing program, record the voice-over into the sequencer program and begin composing. This is an excellent reference tool.

After computing the timings, confirm them with the creatives. What seems logical may not be the agency's vision. A professional announcer can read advertising copy quickly and be perfectly understood. That fact alone could change the final timings. Most agency producers experiment with actors and announcers while either filming or recording, which could change the initial script. Make sure to have the final copy before writing the music.

> If writing to a completed film, it is advisable to check the timing. Sometimes the film might be longer than it should be. The reason (other than a mistake) for this is that the editor cannot fit the appropriate frames into the allotted time. The composer is asked to score to this longer time. After the commercial has been edited, the film company will electronically compress the entire film to fit into the correct time. If the time difference is not too extreme, it will be very difficult to tell that this process has taken place.

The music should not begin until at least seven frames have passed and should end one-half second before the film ends. Time is needed for the video to attain the proper speed at the beginning, and room is needed at the end to cut to another commercial (or program) with a smooth transition.

Ask questions during the initial creative meeting. The following are some suggestions:

Who is the target audience? The answer to this question helps to conjure up musical ideas. For example, if the target audience is fifty- to sixty-five-year-old women, most likely, hip-hop would not appeal to most of them and would therefore be the wrong choice of musical style.

What are the demographics or psychographics of the audience? In this case, the answer helps to narrow musical choices. Within these groups, many styles of music could work; look to the creatives for guidance. It is just as important to know which styles are not acceptable. This should also be a part of the creative discussion.

What style of music works best? It is advisable to bring examples of musical directions to the meeting. Most likely, the creatives will play an example of what they feel would be the appropriate musical style. If a definite musical direction has been chosen, ask if they want the same instrumentation and musical mood as provided in the example. Many times they will like the general feeling of a piece but want the original music to vary from the example; for instance, they might want the original composition to be slower or faster than the example. Make sure the original composition and arrangement are not too close to the example; plagiarism must be avoided. (It is common for the creatives to want the composer to make the original piece as close as possible to the example. In this case, insist that a musicologist examine the composition before the final recording. Many agencies request that the composer sign an agreement absolving the agency from any claim of plagiarism. DO NOT SIGN SUCH AN AGREEMENT!)

Author's Experience: While working on a commercial for the CD-ROM game Elmo's World, based on the *Sesame Street* character, the creatives played a musical example of a simple jazz composition that kept on repeating the same musical phrase. They liked the tempo and instrumentation but not the monotony of the repeated melodic phrase. The first step in analyzing the music was to determine what the creatives liked about the example; they had already revealed what they did not like. The repeated phrase was catchy, and the instrumentation consisted of a rhythm section, with the drummer playing brushes and a vibraphone playing the melody. This instrumentation provided a lively, mellow sound. If the drummer had used sticks and a saxophone had played the melody, the entire character of the composition would have been different.

The first approach was to divide the commercial into sections. The film consisted of an introduction, which suggested writing a musical intro, the heart of the commercial, which suggested a melody, a middle section, which suggested a bridge, and an ending, which suggested a musical ending. Dividing the music into this compositional form kept the essence of the demo (the main melody was a repeated pattern) but eliminated the boredom of only one repeated passage.

Many commercials are analogous to compositional styles that include an introduction, a middle, and an ending. This helps the composer create a cohesive piece of music.

What tempo is most approximate? The tempo is directly related to the creation of a musical mood. If the music is too fast or too slow, the entire feeling of the commercial is changed.

Does the mood of the music have to change within the commercial? Many commercials change moods, and the music will most likely have to change with it. For example, pain reliever commercials (aspirin, etc.) often start with a problem that taking the medication solves. Most of the time in these commercials, the opening music should replicate the uncomfortable feeling and transform into a pleasant section that signifies relief. Even though this seems like an obvious musical choice, the creatives might want only one mood. These are all creative choices and therefore must be discussed. There is no right or wrong.

The music that is suggested by the agency often differs from the composer's initial feel for the music. Since music is a creative choice, many styles will work well.

If there are sound effects, should they be musical or realistic? If a large gun is fired, should the audience hear a deep gunshot or short blast of timpani and low brass playing fortissimo? Realistic or musical effects? The creatives generally know what they want, but the question must still be asked.

What will be the visual look and style of the film? Will it be grainy, shot in color or black and white, edited with fast cuts, traditional or unusual camera angles, and so on? This is difficult to discern when working with a storyboard. Only the creators can answer these questions.

> The agency will frequently request several variations of the same piece of music, or they might approve two separate compositions for the same commercials. After the spot has been filmed, the recorded tracks are added to the video and the final music is chosen.

After a demo has been approved and the final film has been shot, the composer will then adjust the demo to fit the exact timings of the film. After seeing the film, the composer or the creatives might suggest substantial musical changes. Many editors use demos as an editing tool. The ambience of the music helps them with editing decisions. Even after the music has been adjusted, the client might suggest a new edit and/or musical changes. This process usually continues until it is time to send the video to the television stations for airplay.

ANALYZING A STORYBOARD

Let us now analyze an actual storyboard as if we were approaching a real assignment. We will determine the timings from the storyboard and compare them to the actual timings of the final film. Refer to the figure below.

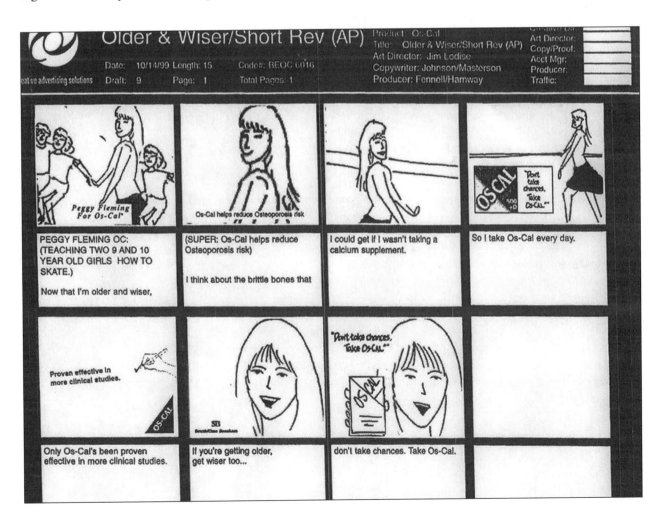

Os-Cal Commercial Campaign

Os-Cal is a pharmaceutical product for women going through menopause. The client chose to do a campaign composed of numerous television commercials. Peggy Fleming, an Olympic gold medalist in ice-skating, was chosen as the spokesperson. She was selected because of her age, her fame, and her beauty; she is an ideal role model for the target audience. (Most women go through menopause between the ages of forty-five and fifty.)

The concept of the commercials was to have Peggy skating (in most of them). This would show how fit she is and how Os-Cal has helped her to avoid osteoporosis by providing enough calcium supplement.

The title of the commercial is "Older and Wiser," and this version runs fifteen seconds (the campaign also included a thirty-second version of the same commercial):

Each timing is a full sentence.

Frame #1 (2 kids on ice, ages 9–12)

Peggy Fleming is skating (her name is superimposed on the screen), and she says, "Now that I'm older,"

Frame #2 (still skating)

"I think about the brittle bones that I could get if I wasn't taking a calcium supplement."

Frame #3

Storyboard timing: 6 seconds

Actual film timing: 5½ seconds

Frame #4 (She points to a poster that says "Don't take chances, take Os-Cal.")

"So I take Os-Cal every day."

Storyboard timing: 2 seconds

Actual film timing: 1 second

Frame #5 (A checkmark is made next to the following text: "Proven effective in more clinical studies.")

This sentence was changed for the film. The film dialogue is:

"Only Os-Cal's been proven effective in more clinical studies."

The timing from the storyboard dialogue was 2 seconds.

The new dialogue was read in two seconds in the final commercial.

Frame #6 (close-up of Peggy's face)

"If you're getting older, get wiser too—"

Frame #7 (Superimposed next to Peggy's face is a picture of the Os-Cal bottle with the words "Don't take chances, take Os-Cal.")

"Don't take chances. Take Os-Cal." (This is the final frame.)

Storyboard timing: 4 seconds

Actual film timing: 4 seconds

The total time of the storyboard reading was 14 seconds; the total time of the final reading on film was 12½ seconds.

If the composer first had to compose to the storyboard, he might have made the mistake of not figuring in the time it took for Peggy Fleming to skate and pause between lines. In the final film, the extra 2½ seconds were spent on Peggy skating and pausing between lines.

The moral of the story is: always allow time for action without dialogue.

ASSIGNMENTS

A professional creative director wrote the following exercise. This is typical of the kind of instructions that are given to a composer prior to shooting the film. In this case, there is no storyboard. Complete the assignment in the time span listed in the instructions.

1. We are shooting a new campaign for XYZ STORES designed to dramatically upgrade the image of the chain.
2. The pictures will be shot by some of the leading fashion photographers, like Helmut Newton and Richard Avidon. The scenes will be shot in New York, London, Paris, and Rome.
3. We will use the best super models, like Cindy Crawford and Naomi Campbell.
4. What we need is a piece of music that will capture it all; the pictures, the attitude, and to really upgrade the XYZ image.
5. I would like the music to be truly memorable—it can be hot and sexy, it could be wonderfully beautiful.
6. The assignment is wide open, and I am open to your ideas. Break ground! Break the rules!
7. People who don't currently shop at XYZ should want to from now on.
8. The spots are 30 seconds, but also come up with something for a 60-second radio.
9. I want to hear demos in three days.

Further exercises:
1. Using a storyboard to work from, lay out a score sheet with "hit" points. These hits should either require effects or mood changes in the music. The objective is to write a cohesive piece of music. Each exercise requires a :30 (30-second) television score.
2. Do an arrangement of your final composition for a small combo.
3. Write two or three different pieces of music, in different styles, for the same commercial. Vary the tempos and moods.

5

Underscoring
(Compositional Techniques)

The main purpose of a commercial is to sell a product. The function of a commercial is to deliver a message explaining why a consumer should purchase that product. Public service commercials give important information, for example, vaccinate children against polio. Image advertising creates goodwill and makes the public aware of a company even though they are not selling a product directly to the consumer, for example, the GE ads that inform the public about products that are not made for the consumer but for use in medicine. Although some commercials may be very creative with wonderful quality film and inspiring music, they may not be good advertising, because they don't have a clear message. Most agencies are trying to accomplish both objectives by combining creative advertising with a clear message.

Music plays a significant role in conveying a commercial message. Writing music to accompany pictures is analogous to solving a puzzle. One piece fits into another until the puzzle is complete. Sometimes the composer has to create a labyrinth of sound; the music weaves in and out until there is some form of conclusion. The difference between a musical puzzle and a conventional puzzle is that the musical puzzle has many ways in which it can be solved. The composer must not only solve the puzzle but also have that solution approved by the client.

The most crucial questions that have to be answered by a composer are:

1. What should the emotional response be from the music?
2. When should the music begin and end?
3. What instrumentation should be used? (This depends on the budget and emotional tone of the film.)

These questions have to be answered and approved by the agency, as do the suggestions of the composer.

HISTORICAL COMPOSITIONAL FORMS

Music comprises melody, harmony, rhythm, variation, arrangement, and orchestration. *The crucial factor in a well-crafted composition is form.* Haphazard writing does not create unity or identity. *Repetition and variation are the most used compositional techniques to create form and symmetry.* This is not to intimate that traditional form must be adhered to in modern popular composition. The value of receiving a traditional musical education is that it gives the composer a background, which has a practical purpose in commercial and film writing.

> A comprehensive musical education exposes the composer to most forms of traditional music. It also provides an opportunity to learn the harmonic and melodic rules of most historical periods. Just as a pianist has to practice in order to become proficient, a composer must compose in order to develop. The more knowledge and technique that is learned, the more the composer has to choose from when approaching an assignment.

Composition is impossible to learn, but what *can* be learned are the "tools" that are available. When master carpenters are making furniture, they use a variety of tools. Through many years of apprenticeship they learn how to master the use of a screwdriver, a saw, a hammer, and so on. The same goes for a well-trained composer; knowledge of harmony, rhythm, melody, and arranging helps to generate and craft a variety of compositional ideas.

Musicians' Brains Wired Differently
By Seth Hettena, Associated Press Writer (2001)

SAN DIEGO (AP)—The brain waves of professional musicians respond to music in a way that suggests they have an intuitive sense of the notes that amateurs lack, researchers said Wednesday. Neuroscientists, using brain-scanning MRI machines to peer inside the minds of professional German violinists, found they could hear the music simply by thinking about it, a skill amateurs in the study were unable to match.

The research offers insight into the inner workings of the brain and shows that musicians' brains are uniquely wired for sound, researchers said at the annual meeting of the Society for Neuroscience.

Neuroscientists often study how we hear and play music because it is one of the few activities that use many functions of the brain, including memory, learning, motor control, emotion, hearing and creativity, said Dr. Robert Zatorre of the Montreal Neurological Institute. "It offers a window onto the highest levels of human cognition," Zatorre said.

In a study by researchers at the University of Tuebingen, the brains of eight violinists with German orchestras and eight amateurs were analyzed as they silently tapped out the first 16 bars of Mozart's violin concerto in G major. Brain scans showed professionals had significant activity in the part of their brains that controlled hearing, said Dr. Gabriela Scheler of the University of Tuebingen. "When the professionals move their fingers, they are also hearing the music in their heads," Scheler said. Amateurs, by contrast, showed more activity in the motor cortex, the region that controls finger movements, suggesting they were more preoccupied with hitting the correct notes, she said. Scheler, a former violinist with the Nuremberg Philharmonic Orchestra, said the findings suggest that professionals have "liberated" their minds from worrying about hitting the right notes. As a result, they are able to listen, judge and control their play, Scheler said. "Presumably, this enhances the musical performance," she said.

In a second experiment, the violinists were asked to imagine playing the concerto without moving their fingers. Brain scans showed again that the professionals were hearing the music in their heads. Zatorre, who has studied the brain's response to music for two decades, said it was the first time anyone had studied music and its relationship to motor control and imagery.

For example, an assignment might be to compose in a certain historical style. Without knowing the melodic, harmonic, and structural rules of that historic period, it is impossible to complete the assignment. The other advantage of having the knowledge is that it gives the composer a grab bag of ideas to choose from. In modern music, historical musical forms have been expanded.

Well-constructed commercials have form. When a composter writes for film, the form she chooses often results from the requirements of the pictures—the pictures dictate the form. It is the job of the composer to create something that is cohesive, even though it may not be traditional. There are many ways in which this can be accomplished, for example, manipulating a short theme, bridging sections with percussion fills or harp glisses, the use of silence, tempo, and key changes.

Something as simple as a two-measure theme can weave itself into something quite interesting, even though it may not be in a traditional form. Just hearing the theme pop up in unusual places with different instrumentation can keep the listener's attention. Many film composers base entire scores on one simple theme that is reinvented in various ways. This compositional device is also effectively used in commercials.

FORM

All forms of modern popular music have developed from traditional musical forms. The following is a list and description of some traditional forms that have been modified and are still used in most styles of music.

Sonata form comes from the classical period and contains three sections: The **exposition** section contains the themes. The **development** section is used to develop and expand the original themes. The use of modulations, themes in retrograde, and inverted and transposed forms are some of the techniques used. Also, the use of fragmented themes is commonly used in commercials. (Using fragmented themes is a commonly used technique in both commercials and films.) The **recapitulation** is a return of the themes of the exposition with some minor changes. The first movement of sonatas, called the allegro, uses this form.

> Recapitulation is used in almost all forms of popular music. The popular song and instrumental composi-
> tions usually repeat the chorus numerous times, which helps the audience remember the chorus; in pop-
> ular music this is referred to as the "hook" of the song. Almost all commercial songs (jingles) have a strong,
> easy-to-remember hook. This helps to create client identity.

Theme and variations is a musical form that dates back to the Baroque and Classical periods. In this technique, a theme is stated, followed by numerous variations of that theme. Some film scores are based on this technique. Varying tempos, keys, time signatures, orchestration, and other compositional devices modifies the original theme.

Binary form has two parts, both of which are usually repeated.

Ternary form has three parts and usually has repeated sections.

A **rondo** consists of a main theme that repeats between several additional sections that vary from the main theme. This form is often used as the final movement of a sonata.

MODERN POPULAR COMPOSITIONAL FORMS

Popular composition is based on traditional form. As in any historical musical time period, those forms are used as a basis and expanded. Popular recorded music is not only based on composition, but the actual production of the music in the studio (application of reverb, delays, etc.) has become as much a part of the composition as the notes. For this reason, having a basic knowledge of music production is relevant to a composer's education and success in this field.

These skills apply to writing music for commercials. Since the majority of assignments are to imitate a popular musical style, the composition must contain the same production values as the recorded musical examples referred to by the agency.

It can be advantageous to keep the following production elements in mind when composing:

Listen to the use of reverberation and echo. Is the snare drum dry (without reverb) or does it have a long de-cay time? Is there a slap echo on the tom-toms (a quick repeat)? Reverberation and echo greatly affect the ambi-ence of the recording.

Listen to the overall level of the most prominent instruments. Is the bass loud in the mix? Is the kick drum as loud as the bass or just felt? Is the overall level of the strings loud or soft in the mix? Certain musical genres have production characteristics, for example, rock and roll has loud guitars, dance music has loud kick drums, hip-hop has loud bass and drums.

Listen to the equalization of each instrument. Does the piano sound warm or thin and percussive? Is the kick drum round and tubby or does it have a hard, pointed sound? Is the sound of the bass round and deep or played with the thumb, which creates a percussive effect?

Equalization (EQ) is a delicate procedure and must be used carefully. Strident, piercing sounds can result from over EQing. Too much low-end can cause distortion.

Listen to the sonic quality and level of the vocals. Does the lead singer sound warm and smooth, or is the equalization on the voice cutting? Is the lead singer doubled in any sections of the song? Are the background singers loud in the mix or much softer than the lead vocal? Are the background vocals doubled or tripled in order to create a full sound? Is there more than one person singing the lead? Are the background vocals used as part of the orchestration by singing syllables instead of words?

The sonic quality of the vocals can have much to do with the choice of microphone. Some microphones sound thin and cutting, whereas others sound warm. A particular microphone used on different singers will have differ-ent sonic results. Experimentation is the only way to make the right choice.

Listen to the sound of the overall mix. Does the mix have an ambience? Many R & B mixes sound dry (very little reverb) with loud and warm sounding vocals. Some of the mixes contain layered background vocals (recorded two or three times) that are prominent in the mix. In many rock and roll mixes, the guitars are louder than the vo-cals. In dance music, the kick drum, hi-hat, and snares are usually prominent.

Listen to the overall instrumentation. If the assignment is to imitate the sound of a particular recording, try to use the same instrumentation. Are most of the sounds from live instruments, synthesized, or a combination? Some musical styles are almost impossible to create on synthesizers—for example, it is difficult to program strumming guitars or rock and roll guitars that sound live. To sound real, guitar strumming requires the feel of a live musician. Other instruments sound quite good on synthesizers. If a string pad is low in the mix, it is difficult to tell that it is not a live string section. (In most commercials, the budget is not large enough to hire a string section.)

Listen to the elements of the arrangement and the orchestration. Since the goal is to imitate a particular sound, the harmonies and general feel of the orchestration must be similar. For example: Are the strings written with closed harmonies, or are the violins playing in a high octave and the remainder of the strings playing a low pad? Is the guitar playing rhythm or playing solo fills? Try to follow the basic format of the musical example.

The assignment might be to write in a certain genre without hearing a specific sample. For example, if the assignment were to write a contemporary hip-hop track, listen to the most popular tracks on the chart and observe common elements. The tempos might range between ninety-five and ninety-eight beats per minute; the tracks might be very sparse; the drum sounds might be sampled from a Roland 909 or 808-drum machine. Observing the most current musical trend will present the composer with a very good basis for completing the assignment successfully.

UNDERSCORING

The term *underscoring* generally refers to instrumental background music that is written to accompany a film; vocals, usually without words, are often used as a part of the orchestration. Many film scores and commercial scores use vocal choruses to add power and richness. The sound and emotion generated by live singers cannot be replaced by synthesized vocals. (Songs used in commercials are referred to as jingles, even though some songwriters resent the term. Jingles will be discussed in a later chapter.)

There is a belief that background music should be "felt and not heard." This means that the score should be unobtrusive and merely accompany the film in such a manner that it provokes the desired emotional response from the audience; if the music from a well-crafted score were removed, the film would lack a key emotional element.

There are many commercials with a minimum of announcer's copy or sparse dialogue. In this scenario, the score is no longer background music but becomes a featured element. This can either help or destroy the effectiveness of the commercial. When the creatives suggest that the composer write a "bed," they are referring to music that is subtle and unobtrusive. If the music is a featured ingredient of the overall commercial, there is usually more time and attention allocated to the composition and production of the music. [Listen to track #9 on the enclosed CD.]

It is obvious when an underscoring does complement the picture. With experience, the composer develops a dramatic sense of what works best with the film. A number of genres might match the film but might not be what the agency wants. Some creatives are very specific, while others do not know what they want until they hear something that feels right.

COMPOSITIONAL PROCEDURE

The compositional techniques used for commercials are similar to those used for film; the main difference is the length of the music. Various techniques will be discussed in this chapter; hopefully this "toolbox" of ideas will be stored in the composer's mind.

> One *major* mistake made by composers is to accept assignments they are not qualified to write. Some composers and arrangers are only skilled in certain styles. If that is the case, they should only accept assignments in those styles. It is very difficult to receive new assignments from an agency that is not satisfied with a previous submission.

After analyzing the film, the first step is to decide on the style of music and have it approved by the agency. Since the average length of a television commercial is thirty seconds, some of the compositional techniques that might apply to a longer composition might not be relevant to commercials; the time for musical development is shorter and therefore limiting. *Economy is the best compositional "tool" for a commercial composer.* This means learning how to expand a flowing composition in a compressed format, which, in many ways, is more difficult than writing a longer composition. The craft can be learned and developed through practice.

The second step is to decide what parts of the film have to be emphasized ("hit") with either musical accents or some form of effect. Take the video counts in frames (where actions occur) and mark them either on the computer sequencer or on the score paper. These counts determine the measure and beat where the accents have to occur at a particular tempo. A change in tempo, obviously, changes the placement of the hit. It becomes more complicated when there is more than one tempo. With modern technology, a computer sequencer program will automatically convert the timings into the proper measure and beats. Example 1 shows hits at different tempos.

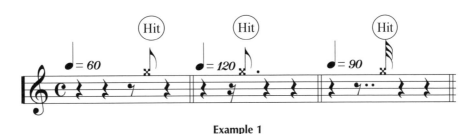

Example 1

When developing music for a commercial campaign, an agency will often request that a theme be composed, submitted, and approved prior to scoring to the film or storyboard. The theme usually must be adaptable to various styles, tempos, and arrangements. Above all, the composition must be a quality piece of music that can be appreciated without seeing the film. The composer should submit at least three themes. If the client and the agency "fall in love" with one of the pieces, the theme must be adaptable. A theme helps to create an identity for the product and therefore must become recognizable in its various versions.

The following are the most common compositional mistakes and should be avoided:

Beginning or ending the music at the wrong time. When writing for television, always begin the music approximately seven frames into the film and finish the music a half-second before the film ends, because at the beginning, it takes time for the video to "roll in" and get up to speed and at the end, time is needed for a smooth transition from the film to the next event. (There are thirty video frames per second.)

Composing a theme that is too long to fit into a shorter version of the same commercial. The most common assignment is to write a thirty-second theme that can be shortened to fifteen seconds. Depending on the musical needs of the film, one suggestion is to write short thematic fragments, which are easily adaptable and lend themselves to modulation, which helps to keep the composition interesting. Another suggestion is to write a theme that is no longer than twelve seconds. This leaves room for an introduction and ending within the fifteen-second commercial and room for expansion in the longer version. (This is based on the tempos of the various versions being the same.) Before writing, experiment with a variety of tempos for the different commercials included in the campaign. It will help determine the flexibility of the theme; not all themes adapt well.

Writing an extended theme that won't work in its original form in all required variations. Sometimes this is a very difficult assignment. In this case, make sure that the first or second part of the theme can be used as an independent theme. This is a common problem when reducing the music to fit into a ten-second version. The theme might work well in a thirty- and fifteen-second version, but there is not enough time to fit the entire piece into nine seconds. If the theme has identifiable sections that can be lifted (edited), try them—this is usually a good solution. Most agencies accept this practice, because they realize that, otherwise, the original composition would have to be compromised to solve the problem. Since most of the airplay will probably be the thirty- and fifteen-second versions, agencies are willing to make this compromise.

Writing themes that are not adaptable to different styles and tempos. Some themes, even though well constructed, are just not adaptable to different styles and tempos. Even though they may fit other styles and tempos, the composition might only sound good in its original form. This problem occurs because, even though the composer might have written a well-constructed theme, she did not check its flexibility. If the theme is going to have to adapt to different versions, experiment with the original before presenting it to the agency. Once the theme has been approved, the integrity of the composition must remain. The agency and client will certainly notice that the theme is missing or incomplete. If the theme has to be compressed for other versions, let the creatives know before writing.

After approving the theme and discussing the various versions, the agency might decide to add another version. If the theme will not fit in its entirety, present the best solution possible and explain the problem to the creatives. Most of the time there is an acceptable solution.

Writing compositions that contain odd time signatures, which could make the rhythm and/or melody feel unnatural. (Rhythm, in this context, does not necessarily refer to drums and percussion but to the flow of the composition.) This normally occurs if the composer wants to start a new musical statement over a particular part of the film. For example, if a scene changes from pictures of mountains to the inside of a department store, the composer will most likely want to start a new section over the new scene rather than continue the previous line. The bar prior to the scene change might require an odd time signature so the timing is correct. There are devices that will help the composer make the composition sound smooth.

Writing in the same frequency range as the actors or the announcer. When scoring to the film, listen closely to the frequency range of the actors' and/or announcer's voices. Frequently, the composition will sound busy and cluttered. One solution is to choose octaves that are far enough away from the frequency range of the voices so as not to conflict. Think of the dialogue as being a part of the orchestration. This also has to be taken into account when writing a theme that runs throughout the commercial. Sometimes sparse writing can be very effective, but there are no rules. Whatever works best is what should be used. (The same principle applies when creating arrangements for vocals.)

> Composers will sometimes write a composition that is too loud and powerful to fit under dialogue without drowning out the actors and/or announcer. They lower the music track during the mixing process in order to achieve the correct balance. The problem with this solution is that, in most instances, the track will be too low to be effective. The most effective solution is to write the music in a less obtrusive manner so that a better balance can be achieved.

COMPOSITIONAL PROBLEMS

Let us assume that the assignment is to compose a melody, a rhythmic groove, and to musically accent the product every time it is shown.

Musically accenting specific events (called "hits") is the most common compositional restriction. For example, let us assume that the picture of the product being advertised instantly appears on the screen in exactly 6½ seconds, lasts 4 seconds, disappears, and the picture then continues with new scenes. Depending on the tempo—referred to as beats per minute, or bpm—the 6½-second mark will appear in different measures and on different beats. For example, if the tempo is 130 beats per minute, the time signature is 4/4, and the hit is at 6½ seconds, the hit would be on the fourth bar, a little after the third beat. If the tempo is 120 bpm, then the 6½-second hit would appear on the fourth bar, directly on the second beat.

Let us also assume that the composition is in 4/4 time, which equals 4 beats per measure, with the quarter note equaling one beat. It is possible that the measure that contains the hit might require a time signature of 3/4 (3 beats per measure), followed by a 2/4 measure (2 beats per measure) and then returning to a consistent 4/4 feel, or 4 beats per measure.

The next information needed is: In what measure and on what beat does the composition resume? For the sake of this exercise, let us assume that it continues on the upbeat of the first beat following a 2/4 measure. Example 2 shows multiple meter changes.

This scenario presents a creative problem. What devices can the composer use to make the composition flow instead of sounding choppy and unnatural? The answer to this question depends on the nature of the composition prior to the hit. We know (from the assignment) that there must be a flowing melody and it has to lead into the product shot, which will require some form of an effect. We also know that the composition has a percussive engine propelling the track. One solution might be to keep the percussive pattern throughout the hit and have the

Example 2

melody end just before the hit and then lead into the next section with a percussion fill, which is a normal device used to connect one section to another. When a groove is continuous, even though the time signature might vary, the groove will, most likely, continue to sound natural. Another solution might be to merely have a sudden stop where the hit occurs, play the effect for the product shot, followed by a drum pickup, which brings it back into the groove.

Depending on the melodic structure, it is sometimes possible to add extended note durations or subtract durations in order to meet the needs of the film. For example, if the time signature did not change and the melody note was a quarter note, one beat short for the following hit, try extending the quarter note to a half note, which allows the next section of the melody begin on the hit. This solution does not always create a flowing, natural-sounding melody. It sometimes requires a restructuring of the melody.

There are many possible solutions to this problem and similar compositional problems. These examples are offered so the student can understand how to approach a similar situation. Experimentation will generally bring a satisfactory solution.

COMPOSITIONAL TECHNIQUES

There are certain techniques that can help determine an initial compositional style for a commercial. With experience, the composer will develop many "tools" that will generate compositional ideas.

Choose a theme for each character. Some commercials have several actors. If time permits, a short theme can be written for each character. This creates a musical identity. One the most commonly used commercial formats is the vignette.

Sample Vignette
In the first vignette a woman standing in her kitchen says:
"I have been getting headaches for years."
In the second vignette a man sitting at his desk says:
"The stress of my job gives me headaches."
In the third vignette a college student in his dorm room says:
"Exams give me a headache."

Let us assume that it takes each actor four seconds to say his or her line. If there is a short theme that repeats in a modulated form each time a line is spoken, the audience will relate the theme to each situation. Repeating the theme modulating to different keys keeps it from becoming boring. This is a commonly used device and can be effective.

The theme, generally, has to be simple in order not to conflict with the voices. A short theme at the end of each line—which bridges with the next vignette—works well. How well it works depends on how much talking there is in each vignette. Experiment! Many film composers use this technique; it is more easily applied to longer spots. Example 3 is an excerpt from Piano Concerto in A minor by Grieg.

Silence is as important as notes. Inexperienced composers tend to overwrite. They think that the music must be constant or there will be a lull. This is not true. Silence can be one of the most affective compositional techniques; it can create a dramatic mood or just a surprise, in any genre.

Example 3

Let us assume that a commercial depicts the horrors of drugs. The last scene is a picture of a dead body, the result of a drug overdose. If the music stops on the shot of a casket, silence will create a dramatic moment.

Starting the music halfway into the film can also be affective. If you decide to do this, get approval from the creatives. They are usually quite specific about where they want the music to begin.

Ostinatos create tension. Ostinatos (repeated musical patterns), with various sounds weaving in and out, tend to create a feeling of tension. Ostinatos are frequently heard in pain reliever commercials. At the beginning, the patient has a headache, and after she consumes the product, the pain goes away. The patient is then portrayed as living an active life. Many of the scores accompanying the headache scenes contain ostinatos with dark-sounding elements that add to a feeling of discomfort; when relief comes, the ostinatos are replaced with uplifting, pleasant music.

There are musical patterns that help to create different emotions. One of the advantages of using some of these patterns is that, if used properly, the patterns become "catchy" (easy to remember), which increases audience identity. There is such a short time to establish an identity that these "tools" (e.g., catchy bass patterns, repeated guitar, and piano riffs) are certainly worth investigating.

Taking a nontraditional approach to the music can be interesting. This is usually referred to as "going against the picture"—writing music that is unexpected.

> The author worked on a commercial for Master Lock, which was specifically filmed for the Super Bowl. The picture showed a burglar trying to break a lock without success. The traditional approach would have been to write something dark, electronic, or cinematic; actually many styles would have complemented the picture and worked well. Instead, the agency wanted a calm piece of classical music. The final choice was to use a calm, mellow, vocal serenade sung in German and composed by Mozart; it was a totally unexpected marriage of film and music. The commercial was hailed as an outstanding spot on the Super Bowl and received much notoriety in advertising circles, one of the main reasons being that the music was in juxtaposition to the picture.
>
> It was a difficult assignment from several viewpoints. The first concern was to not destroy a great piece of music by having to fit it into a thirty-second commercial. The solution was to find a harmonically acceptable edit point that would make the composition sound as if it had not been edited. After much experimentation with the orchestration, a smooth transition was accomplished.
>
> The second concern was to hire an orchestra that would play Mozart in the authentic style, and a third concern was to hire an opera singer who had sung Mozart. All items were accomplished. This is a good example of ways to make the music as authentic as possible.

The musical approach is usually suggested by the agency and is an intrinsic part of the original concept of the commercial. Never go against the picture without approval from the agency. If warranted, make a specific suggestion to the creatives; it might spur some creative thinking.

Since contemporary popular music is mostly rhythm based, it can be advantageous to approach a composition by developing a rhythm pattern as the first step. Know the style of music before writing a rhythm pattern. Let us assume that the agency wanted a Latin pop rhythm. The next question would be, "There are many kinds of Latin-Hispanic rhythms. What Latin style would you like?—Caribbean (denotes congas), maracas playing Afro-Cuban rhythms (denotes a mixture of African and Cuban rhythms), traditional Mexican (requires mariachi trumpets and acoustic guitars, including the Mexican bass guitar which looks like a guitar), and so on." Once the desired style has been determined, try writing a two- or four-measure loop (repeated pattern) and play it against the film. Even without hearing a melodic structure, it will be easy to tell if the feel of the rhythm fits. The next step could be to try developing a rhythm pattern with appropriate breaks and fills to fit the different sections of the film. Then try experimenting with melodic lines, a bass or piano part, or just experiment until a kernel of an idea feels good; continue developing and adjusting all of the elements. Eventually, you will have an interesting piece of music.

Working with a rhythm pattern does not necessarily mean that the rhythm has to be played by percussion instruments. Orchestras can play rhythm patterns; pianos, basses, and strings can all play rhythm patterns. For example, ostinatos are rhythmic patterns and can be played by most orchestral sections.

> An interesting approach to rhythm-based composition is to notate rhythm patterns without filling in the notes or the instruments that would play them—just write Xs. Then begin experimenting with instruments and notes playing those patterns. Some interesting compositions have been created using this technique. Try experimenting with instruments other than percussion to begin a composition. For example, start with only a piano, which helps to define the harmony. Listen to the piano against the film. If it feels good, keep adding parts and developing the composition and the arrangement. One of the dangers of using this technique is not being able to expand the orchestration; instruments other than the piano might sound better on a part that had been originally played on the piano. Whenever composing on an instrument, be very careful not to limit the composition by the inherent limitations of that instrument or the technical limitations that the composer might have in his ability to play that instrument well. Always try to hear as much as possible of the composition and orchestration internally and then assign it to the appropriate instrument. This point has been made before, but it is important to keep in mind, because this kind of limitation hinders many young composers.
>
> One of the advantages of working with synthesizers is that it is possible to hear what real instruments would sound like without having to pay musicians during the experimental stage. Once the piece has been demonstrated on synthesizers to the agency and approved, hire the live musicians—if needed—to replace some of the synthesized parts. Synthesized guitars and horns do not generally sound real enough. If the budget is small and the desired sound is a horn section, add one real horn to the synthesized section; it is surprising how real one live player can make a synthesized part sound. This technique also works well with strings.
>
> Synthesized sounds have become so popular, and many of them are not supposed to sound real; these are referred to as analog sounds. The synthesizer programmer, through experimentation, usually programs sounds. The sounds that can be generated are infinite. Genres, such as trance, most dance music, and electronica, are examples of musical styles that usually do not include live musicians; also, most electronic effects are created with analog sounds. Because analog is so popular, it behooves the composer to learn how to program or, if not, hire an inventive programmer.

Electronics has changed the way commercial composers conceive of music. Most compositions used in commercials are played by a combination of live musicians and synthesizers. Electronic music not only samples (digitally records) and plays back real-sounding instruments (samples) but also has a musical language of its own (as previously described in the explanation of analog synthesis).

Because of the available technology, the composer has been able to conceive of and hear almost any sound imaginable.

- If a "musical bed" (sustained chords) were desired, one of the traditional orchestral approaches would be to use a string section. By having synthesizers available, the composer can combine three or four richly textured sounds to replace the traditional string section; not only will the part sound rich and full, but it will also have a texture different from that of a real string section.
- Creating an ostinato with an analog sound is very effective. Ostinatos can create musical tension or provide a beautiful underlying counterpart to a floating melody.
- Generating a bass part using an analog bass sound is popular in contemporary recordings. Because sounds can be edited and/or created using synthesis, the varieties of sounds are infinite.

> Because of the ever-changing musical trends in commercial music (as previously stated), "sounds" also become trends. Always be aware of the current contemporary markets and stay familiar with the ever-changing technology.

After becoming familiar with synthesis, the composer will begin to think of abstract sounds as an intrinsic part of the composition.

Computers have changed the way music is conceived and composed. Aside from the popularity and public acceptability of synthesis, the major contribution to the music industry has been the flexibility that computers have provided. Numerous edits and experimentation can be accomplished with the flick of a button. Before computers, this process would have taken hours and been costly.

> One of the problems that arise as a result of the computer's flexibility is that the agencies sometimes take advantage of the composers by asking for numerous edited versions of a composition. What they do not realize is that editing does not just require cutting and pasting sections together. Most changes in compositions require some form of restructuring in order to sound cohesive musically and technically. Even if only one measure has to be adjusted, it is still time consuming for several reasons. Because of the many effects that can be applied during programming, editing can create technical problems. For example, if a sustain pedal was open on the last note of the measure where an edit was going to take place, after the new section was spliced to that measure, the sustain pedal would still be open, causing a mishmash of sound. The programmer has to look at the problem and solve it by adjusting the length of time the sustain pedal is open. Similar problems occur with reverbs and other effects. These adjustments can be time consuming without the benefit of additional remuneration. There is really nothing that can be done about this problem because of the competition to get jobs. There will always be someone who is willing to do the extra work.

The use of effects (whether real sound effects or abstract sounds created with synthesizers) has become a major compositional technique since the advent of synthesizers. Before the common use of synthesizers, specialists called Foley artists created sound effects; in recent years, in addition to the creation of effects by Foley artists, many sound effects have been recorded on CDs and then matched and transferred to film. Today, it is rare to have a Foley artist work on a commercial—the composer is expected to add the sound effects. Foley artists are still used in motion pictures. There are Foley stages at motion picture studios that are designed to have Foley artists create live effects, for example, footsteps, clothes rubbing together, and so on. Foleying helps to add the ambient sounds of a scene that were not picked up by the live microphones on the set.

Using synthesized sound effects has helped to create a form of composition known as sound design. (In films, sound design means sound effects specialists—not music.) Sound design generally refers to a composition that does not have a melody, contains numerous synthesized and/or real effects, and, more often than not, has a complex rhythm track. Some commercials have only effects and no music. Even though there is no music, this form of sound design can create a certain rhythm, but not in the traditional sense; the cumulative effect is a rhythmic pace. A dance genre called industrial is based on this premise. Sound design can be one of the most creative tools of the composer. Using sound design, a composer can work without restrictions and get as creative as possible. Sound design can be created in any genre of music, not just the most current trends.

Sound design has also become popular in film scoring. The primary difference is that most films employ Foley artists and the composer does not usually have to design the real sound effects. Big-budget films generally have extensive use of sound designers who use both synthesized and Foley effects. Sound design is especially prevalent in movie trailers. In almost any action movie, the sound design is a major element in the film. Sometimes, well-produced sound design contributes to the ultimate success of the film. For example, in the film *Pearl Harbor*, if the attack had not been accompanied by exciting sound design, the movie might not have been as successful as it was. With the sophisticated sound systems that are in most modern theaters (surround sound), the dialogue, music, and effects are as important as the acting, writing, direction, and the general cinematic quality of the film. [Listen to tracks #1 and #10 on the enclosed CD.]

> When composing and arranging in modern forms of popular music, the composer has to be aware of the changing sounds used primarily in the drum, bass, and keyboard parts. Because of the popularity of synthesizers in records, sounds of various instruments become trendy. For example, the most used sounds for drums in dance music have emanated from two vintage drum machines—the Roland 808 and the Roland 909. Many manufacturers have sampled the sounds, edited them, and included them on sampling CDs and as part of a collection of sounds included in synthesizers that play samples. For many years, the Moog syn-

thesizer has been a staple in creating very deep and rich bass sounds. There are many variations of Moog bass sounds. A Wurlitzer electric piano sound, as opposed to a Rhodes electric sound, has become the standard electric piano in chill-out (also known as down tempo) music.

Commonly used phrases and rhythms in certain styles of music also become trends. For example, a sixteenth-note drum fill that crescendos at the end of an eight-bar phrase has become a signature in various styles of dance music. A kick drum that plays four quarter notes in each bar (called four-on-the-floor) is the standard pattern for house dance music.

As previously discussed in the section dealing with authenticity, the composer working in popular music must keep abreast of the technical and instrumental trends and keep changing with them. If dealing in currently popular music, the composer will be considered dated, if he or she is not up on the latest sounds and technology.

Musical logos are designed as a form of product identity. Most commercials end with a product shot. It is sometimes helpful to suggest that a musical logo be played over this shot. The logo is especially effective if there is a campaign and the logo can be used at the end of each commercial. This technique establishes a musical thread throughout the campaign. Sometimes the agency asks for logos to be sung. This subject will be covered in the chapter dealing with jingles.

Featuring a solo instrument can sometimes bring an immediate identity to a commercial. Before using this technique, discuss it with the creatives; play them a sample of the instrument before writing. This is a specific concept and must be approved.

The synthesized sound for the theme of the television program *The X-Files* is a good example. The composer experimented extensively before choosing that sound. The theme has a unique and memorable quality. The use of unusual instruments, e.g., panpipes and ethnic instruments, also helps to achieve unique sounds.

When the story of a commercial requires a change in the musical mood, it is sometimes affective to change the music before the new scene appears. The audience will then subliminally anticipate a mood change.

Let us assume that the beginning of the film shows a new car sitting in traffic with horns honking, drivers with road rage, and pedestrians crossing the street in front of cars. The car then reaches the open highway, and a feeling of freedom occurs. If the music evokes the confusion at the beginning and the mood shifts to a feeling of freedom, one technique is to start the change of music one or two beats before the change of scene. This technique is commonly used in film music.

Sometimes just a suitable piece of music, with no hits, is the correct choice. The mood produced by the music can be enough to create the correct emotional response to the film. This approach gives the composer a chance to write without restrictions. This is a common technique in writing film music.

MUSIC DEMOS

Many agencies hire several individual composers or music houses to submit demos for a commercial or a commercial campaign. The success of the demos determines who gets the job. As a general rule, try to submit three pieces of music:

1. Write what the creatives ask for.
2. Write what you want to write (assuming you have a different conception than the creatives).
3. Write additional music that is in a different musical direction than the other pieces.

There are several reasons for submitting at least three demos:

1. The agency will request several demos.
2. The composer has a better opportunity to satisfy the creatives by submitting various styles. One of the submissions might be unexpected and be the one chosen.

3. Submitting more than one example improves the chances of being selected for the assignment.

> Submitting too many demos can work against a composer. Some music companies submit six or seven demos. This can be perceived as the composer not fully understanding the assignment and therefore fishing for the right result. The best strategy is to submit the strongest three compositions.

DEMO PRODUCTION

In general, the musical and technical quality of demos has to be that of a finished track. Before the advent of synthesizers, composers would generally play or record a demo on the piano or guitar, and that was usually the extent of auditioning a composition.

Synthesizers enable a composer to present completed or almost completed tracks without having to hire too many musicians, which is costly. Because of this practice, agencies have come to expect master quality demos, while only paying minimum demo fees.

> Developing an expertise with synthesis is essential to being successful in writing for commercials. Most composers have extensive synthesizer workstations and have become, out of necessity, competent engineers. Most music houses will not hire composers who don't have these skills.

Usually, the winning composition requires revisions. The following are some of the reasons revisions might be needed:

Sometimes demos are written to work prints. A work print is not the final film but, usually, a work in progress. A work print is almost always revised, which also requires a revision in the music.

The agency might suggest adding or deleting hits. If the hits are in the form of effects, they can sometimes be added to the mixed music track; if the hits are in the form of composition, then the piece has to be revised and rerecorded.

It is always advisable to ask the creatives if they want realistic effects added. Do not assume anything.

> Many hours were spent adding sound effects to a commercial for Elmo's World (a computer game for kids). However, the effects had to be deleted, because it is illegal to portray effects that are not included on the game's soundtrack. The law states that there must be truth in advertising.

There are some exceptions with regard to how complete a demo has to sound:

Sometimes the director wants a rhythmic groove to play on the set; it helps to create a mood for the actors. In this case, a complete track is not necessary. It is advisable to create several grooves, which enables the director to experiment on the set.

An editor may want a rhythm track to edit to; it creates a pace or mood. There can be a danger in submitting a rhythm track that is used in editing the final track; if the agency or composer wants to change the tempo or feel, there could be creative problems; for example, the track may not sound good at the new tempo. Most of the time, there are solutions.

> Some commercials have a film that only runs approximately twenty-five seconds, more or less, and four-second local tags are added at a later time. Ask the creatives if they want a full twenty-nine and one-half seconds of music or if they want the music to end with the film. Sometimes, they will ask for a separate musical tag (musical ending) to finish the commercial. The tag might be used on numerous spots of the same advertising. An example of a singing tag/logo is "G.E., We Bring Good Things to Life."

A simple piano or guitar track might be adequate for a first submission. This is ordinarily acceptable when an agency is exploring ideas and the budget is modest. Once a musical direction has been chosen, there is usually an ample demo budget.

A simple demo is not recommended if there is an option. The chances are that even at the beginning stages of selecting music, there will be competition. Most music companies present finished-sounding demos.

CONCLUSION

Compositional "tools" are merely aids. The most important element is creativity, which cannot be taught. Initially, always write what you feel. If the agency disagrees with your musical approach, they will tell you. Most composers cannot explain why they have written a certain piece of music. They usually say, "It just feels right."

ASSIGNMENT

Tape a commercial. Choose a musical mood (e.g., gentle, high energy, etc.) and write three demos, all different, but keeping within the feeling of the chosen mood. Experiment by completing several mixes of each composition, trying to create different moods by using creative technology. [Listen to track #12 on the enclosed CD.]

6

Arranging and Orchestration Concepts
(Including Sound Effects and Sound Design)

> The music, however great or small, is what there is to say. The orchestration is how you say it.
>
> —Robert Russell Bennett

Note: The words *arranger* and *orchestrator* will be used interchangeably in this chapter. This section is not devoted to basic arranging and basic orchestration but rather to a discussion of how to achieve an overall instrumental texture. It is assumed that the student already has some basic arranging knowledge. Even if the student lacks this knowledge, an understanding of the concepts is essential in order to guide an arranger or orchestrator in achieving his musical goal. Furthermore, since we are dealing primarily in commercial music, we will focus more on the use of synthesizers than orchestral instruments. Most commercial productions use a combination of synthesizers and live musicians. Rock and roll, gospel, and jazz pieces primarily consist of live musicians using synthesizers as one an adjunct.

Arranging is the art of taking a composition and giving it a musical setting. This includes the harmonies, the basic rhythmic feel (which is usually indicated), and the notes to be played. **Orchestration** is the art of assigning instruments to each note so that the arrangement can be heard. (The term *orchestration* is most often used when describing the process of assigning the notes to an orchestra or other instrumental combination.)

Arranging and orchestrating are analogous to painting. A painter has a palette from which he chooses and mixes colors. Arrangers/orchestrators have a palette upon which they store notes, harmonies, rhythms, instruments, and dynamics. Painters and arrangers/orchestrators mix colors and use different brushes and strokes to produce a final result. Talent and taste are what determine the quality of the work.

The twentieth-century English composer Vaughan Williams studied with the great romantic composer Ravel. Ravel's main contribution to Vaughan Williams's style was teaching him orchestration. He taught him "how to orchestrate in points of color rather than lines" (Grout, *A History of Western Music*, 695). This was also Debussy's philosophy.

This concept is the one used by orchestrators writing for film. Since the composer has to be cautious not to interfere with the dialogue, the orchestration has to complement the film through tonal colors.

Studying the work of the masters adds knowledge to the creative "tool" box. Studying their orchestrations and compositions generates ideas.

In most commercial music (excluding motion pictures and Broadway shows) the arranger and orchestrator are usually the same person. In film scores and Broadway shows, there is usually a separate orchestrator because of time restrictions.

Most film composers write their scores on six to ten staves (like an expanded piano part) with instrumental indications, e.g., "flute to play_____, violins play _____," etc. Most Broadway scores are detailed, two-stave piano parts and in some cases contain orchestral indications, e.g., "trumpet plays_____," etc.

Many orchestrators of commercial music not only assign the notes to instruments but also enhance the arrangements. Because of time restrictions, the composer will indicate what to fill in, e.g., "add a jazz drum part." Sometimes the lead saxophone part is written and the indication is to "fill in the harmonies."

Arranging and orchestrating for the studio are more complex than writing for a live performance. The main difference is the manner in which the sound can be manipulated. The arranger has time to address minute details that are inherent to the recording process. Each recorded track can have its own automated EQ and effects. Throughout a recording, the parameters of the sound can continually change through the use of automation. Also, because of the control over instrumental balance, unusual instruments can be featured. Many of these instruments would not be heard in a traditional live acoustical setting without painstaking manipulation.

APPROACHING THE SCORE

Begin by writing a simple sketch of the layout of the arrangement; include chord symbols, to help map out the harmony. It is helpful to use the top line of the score paper as an overall guide. Write the melody, chord symbols, and lyrics and/or dialogue. Once this has been completed, begin writing the arrangement. Use the following outline as a guide.

Lay out the score paper with the proper key signature for each instrument (if writing a transposed score) and indicate the name of each instrument. If the score is for a traditional orchestra or band, some paper manufacturers provide paper with the instruments printed on it. It is best to use paper that has eight measures per page. Score paper that has only four measures per page can become bulky and difficult for the conductor to follow.

Some composers write sketches and give them to an orchestrator for completion. Composers work in different ways. Some do very detailed sketches using eight or more staves, while others only use two or four staves. They usually indicate the suggested instrumentation for the orchestrator to follow.

Many composers will record the composition using synthesizers; this serves as a detailed guide for the orchestrator. Some composers watch a MIDI notation computer program while recording an orchestra. (The notation program displays the MIDI notes as regular notation manuscript.) The composer can then be certain that the orchestrator has been accurate. This also serves as a way to save time in the recording studio. It is easier to make changes.

Some arrangers write a full sketch of the arrangement and then orchestrate it themselves. This generally depends on the amount of time they have to complete the project. Traditionally, arranging commercials has a very fast turnaround period and there is not enough time to write out an entire sketch. Most arrangers who write on synthesizers will program the arrangement rather than write it out. They then print the notation program that comes with most MIDI sequencer programs.

Some arrangers write in concert key. The author prefers writing in concert, especially for a large orchestra. It is easier to "see" the harmonies and find mistakes quickly. If writing in concert, be familiar with the proper transpositions. In the studio, transposition must be done instantly.

Some arrangers prefer transposing while writing. They think that by seeing the same notes the player reads, it is easier to tell if the parts look generic to the instrument—not consistently too high or too low for a particular instrument.

Each section should have traditional rehearsal markings. Mark each main section with a letter, e.g., A, B, C, and each measure with a number, e.g., 1, 2, 3. This saves time in the studio, because the conductor can communicate using the rehearsal markings.

Be precise with dynamic markings and all other musical indications. The cost of being in the studio prohibits wasting unnecessary time. Plan as much as possible before the session.

Technological advances have enabled live performances to emulate recordings. This is accomplished in several ways:

1. Some acts play prerecorded tracks along with the live performance. This enhances the fullness and ambience of the sound. Frequently, they play the tracks used on the original recording.

2. Individual parts are preprogrammed on a computer-sequencing program and played in synchronization with the live performance. The drummer wears headsets and hears a metronome-like "click track," along with the music, which aids in keeping time with the computer tracks.

3. Small-scale productions of Broadway shows will sometimes have additional parts programmed on synthesizers, for example, horns and strings. This technique is frequently used on cruise ships.

Elements to be considered when creating an arrangement:

The format. Are the verses and choruses in the proper order? This is the job of the composer or jingle writer and the music producer. The lyric writer, when composing jingles, usually determines the format. If the format does not seem musical, make suggestions on how to improve it.

Rhythm. After determining the basic rhythm feel, the arranger should play a sample for the creative people. The "feel" of the composition is the first element of the arrangement. This is usually predetermined, but there are still creative choices that will vary between arrangers.

Harmony. Some composers only submit a lead sheet to the arranger. A typical lead sheet consists of a lead melody, lyrics, and chord symbols. The arranger has many options when choosing how to harmonize the arrangement. Some arrangers like to add chord substitutions in order to add variety to the arrangement. Do not do this without permission. Some substitutions can change the character of the composition, and the creatives will not hear what they approved. Play examples for the creatives before completing the arrangement.

Instrumentation. This is generally determined before the arrangement is written. Since the arranger will usually have some fresh ideas once the creative process begins, they should be discussed with the creative people. Budget is always a consideration.

The arrangement and orchestration create the mood and musical colors of the composition. The texture of the entire composition rests in the hands of the arranger once the composition has been approved. Have specific conversations dealing with this issue.

The key contributes to the ambience of the entire composition. Different keys can evoke different moods. In one key, the first note may be an E above middle C; in another key, the first note may be a B above middle C—much higher; this will obviously change the tessitura, which will affect the entire sound. The key is crucial and should be considered an important factor while creating the arrangement. This has to be discussed with the composer.

When arranging vocals, make certain the key is correct before arranging. Call the singer(s) and confirm that the key will be comfortable. If they arrive at the session and the key is wrong, it might be too late to make adjustments. When the entire program is synthesized, changing the key is simple; if there is a live orchestra, it will be very difficult, unless it is a simple transposition.

> Ensuring that the key is correct for the singers is the responsibility of the composer, and if there has to be a rerecording because of key problems, the additional expense will come out of the music company's budget. Since recording the final music for commercials is usually the last element before the final film mix, there will be time problems if there has to be a rerecord. An error like this, which is easily avoidable, can damage the relationship between the composer and the music house.

Keys effect voicings. If a key is changed after the arrangement has been completed, pay particular attention to the transposed voicings. Some may sound too high and some too low and muddy. Usually, inversions have to be adjusted when there is a key change.

Tempo helps to establish the mood. A change of just two metronome markings can transform the entire mood of a piece. Sometimes, for technical reasons (e.g., the piece might not fit into the proper time at the original tempo when adjusting it to the final film), the original tempo marking has to change. If the creative people do not want to change the film so that the original tempo will work, play them the new tempo so they know what to expect in the studio.

Sound effects. Both musical and real sound effects can add an interesting and unique sound. Consider the sound effects as part of the composition; otherwise, the effects can sometimes mask the music. [Listen to track #7 on the enclosed CD.]

> Overbearing sound effects are a major thorn in the side of film composers. Since film composers do not create the effects, they sometimes do not get to hear them until the film has been mixed. Loud effects can

muddy entire cues. Unfortunately, this is the director's choice, and all a composer can do is voice an objection.

Modulation can heighten the arrangement. Modulations, either up or down, greatly contribute to the mood. This is directly related to the previous discussion on how the key affects the mood. Modulating can be affective when used properly and annoying when not.

Singers singing syllables create a unique sonority when used as apart of the orchestra (e.g., *Star Wars*, *Spider Man* scores). Choruses are frequently used in film scores. They can bring a remarkable contribution to the overall sound of the orchestration. (The use of choruses in commercials is unusual because of the cost.)

Solo instruments can add interest and variation. Composer John Williams used solo violin, played by Itzhak Perlman, as the featured instrument throughout the score of *Schindler's List*. Composer Tan Dun featured solo cello, played by Yo-Yo Ma, in the soundtrack to *Crouching Tiger, Hidden Dragon*.

Using unusual instruments can create timbres that will draw attention to the music, for example, the Arabic oud (like a mandolin) or nay (a wooden flute that has a beautiful expressive sound).

Some dance music arrangers record looped tracks (repeated patterns) and then mute tracks, turn them back on, and edit sections as a way of creating an arrangement. This concept can be applied to certain kinds of commercials, mainly groove-oriented music.

APPROACHING AN ARRANGEMENT

Most composers envision the arrangement and relate their concept to the arranger. Become familiar with the particular genre of music. Listen to the radio and listen to CDs that contain music with a similar arranging concept. The Internet is also a good source for research. Most record buying sites on the Internet allow the consumer to listen to preview samples.

> If the assignment were to compose and arrange a hip-hop track, it might be beneficial to listen to a hip-hop drum loop while composing. This would help to create the proper ambience and lay a foundation for the arrangement. The arranger has a certain goal, and the more specific the assignment, the better chance of pleasing the creative team.

If the arranger is not the same person as the composer, the arranger probably will not be dealing directly with the agency but with the composer. This makes it easier because the composer can communicate in specific musical terms. The arranger should ask questions before beginning to work. The following is a list of suggested questions:

Do the creatives want the same instrumentation as the example or demo? If the example is orchestral, for instance, the budget may not allow for the same number of musicians. Any problems similar to this should be explained to the creatives before beginning work.

How many musicians can be hired within the allotted budget? Be certain to allow for the proper number of musicians in the initial budget proposal.

Will the arrangement have to be edited to fit time lengths other than the original? The agency will often request a fifteen-second version of a longer arrangement. This has an effect on how the original arrangement is created. If the arranger has prior knowledge that the arrangement will need editing, it helps to create the arrangement with easy edit points. Sometimes it is necessary to rerecord because the edited version will not match the picture.

USING TECHNOLOGY

There are numerous ways to accomplish a desired "sound." In the section titled Studio Technology as It Applies to Music Production, in chapter 3 (p. 29), there was a discussion that dealt with the importance of using technology in a creative way. In all forms of commercial music, technology is involved in the creative process of arranging and orchestrating. The use of equalization, as well as effects such as reverberation, echo, delays, flangers, choruses, compressors, limiters, and the infinite number of variations of these basic effects units, enters into the creative process.

If the arrangement requires a rhythm section, a string section, and a horn section (performed by live musicians), internalize the sound and feel of the arrangement. Do not rely on an instrument, for example, a keyboard or a guitar, to help in the writing. The composer's technical limitations on that instrument might hinder the creative process.

Considerations

Rhythm Section

Should the bass be acoustic or electric? If electric, should it be a bass guitar with frets, or fretless? The sound is different. Most jazz players use a fretless bass, whereas most rock players prefer a bass with frets.

Should the guitar be acoustic or electric? There are many kinds of electric guitars; be specific when hiring a player. If an acoustic guitar is desired, should the sound be that of nylon strings or steel strings? Should the guitar have twelve strings or six strings? All of these factors affect the overall sound of the arrangement.

How should the drums be tuned? For example, should the snare drum have a tight high sound or a deep sound? Should the bass drum sound tight and dead or have a deep thump?

String Section

How large a section can be hired within the budget? How should the section be divided, i.e., the number of violins, violas, celli, and basses? The larger the section, the richer the sound will be.

Assuming that the budget allows for six string players, arrangers use different combinations, depending on the needs of the arrangement. If the section is small, some arrangers might only use violins; others might use three violins, two violas, and one cello, while others might hire four violas, one cello, and one double bass. There are no rules. The creative arranger will know the best combination for the particular arrangement.

Horn Section

The instrumentation depends on the sound of the arrangement. Let us assume the budget allows for six players. If the arrangement is supposed to sound exciting, the arranger might use two trumpets, one tenor trombone, and one alto, one tenor, and one baritone saxophone. There are many combinations that will produce the desired result. Let the arranger determine the most appropriate combination.

THE RHYTHM SECTION

The rhythm section is the backbone of most popular music arrangements. Generally, the rhythm section consists of keyboards, guitar, bass, drums, and percussion. The arranger must become familiar with the various choices of instruments offered in each category. Each instrument will be discussed in more detail later in this chapter.

One of the main differences between traditional arranging and arranging in a popular musical style is that most arrangers want the rhythm section to sound loose and expressive instead of only playing the part exactly as written. For this reason, arrangers usually use rhythm section parts as guides and instruct the players to "open up the parts" and add their individuality. If musicians did not bring a unique element to their playing, an arranger could hire almost any player who could read music. This is definitely not the case in popular music. The same principle applies to synthesizer programmers; each programmer brings individuality to her programming and develops trademarks in precisely the same manner as live musicians like Louis Armstrong and Kenny G. Many programmers spend as much time programming and developing sounds as they do working on the arrangement. It once again becomes the *creative use of technology.*

Since computer sequencers first became popular, one of the most frequently used features was quantizing, which corrects the timing of a part that is played or programmed into a sequencing program. For example, the notes could be quantized, which moves them to the closest eighth note or sixteenth note; a swing feel could be added, or the snare drum could purposely sound behind the beat—"laid back." The result could be a very precise but stiff-sounding part. Most programmers now place some of the tracks either before or after the beat, in order to achieve a more live feeling. Creating a specific feel might require that some of the parts be precisely quantized and other parts be moved before or after the beat. Experimentation is the only method of achieving the proper feeling.

The rhythm section should be heard as a tightly knit unit. This can be accomplished in several ways:

If the parts are synthesized, solo each instrument and check for mistakes. Make certain that the part has been properly quantized. That the quantizing is technically correct does not necessarily mean that the particular quantized setting (eighth note, sixteenth note, swing feel, etc.) is the most appropriate for the composition. For example, the arranger might decide to quantize the entire track with a swing feel; within the swing feel option there are suboptions. It is analogous to the links that are available from one website to another. Also, check for notation mistakes within the MIDI program. Because there are extreme velocity changes within a MIDI program, it is sometimes difficult to hear a mistake unless the track is soloed.

Most sequencer programs offer numerous choices within most editing parameters. Through the use of automation, parts can be edited throughout the composition to help accomplish the best feel for each section. As with everything else in music, there are no rules. It once again becomes the *creative use of technology*.

Solo each section and solo various combinations. If each part does not feel good as an individual part or as a part within a section, there is something wrong—rework the part. Even if the parts sound like they fit together when you're listening to the arrangement as a whole, with closer scrutiny, you'll notice that something does not quite feel right.

Making sure that the track "feels good" should be RULE NUMBER ONE when arranging popular music.

If acoustic instruments are recorded into a digital audio program, solo each instrument and check for mistakes. Since the parts will appear as acoustic waveforms, the waveforms can be edited. Digital editing is advantageous because not only can parts be corrected and effected (gated, reverberation, etc.), but they can be edited numerous times without any loss of audio quality. As a safety precaution, solo each track before releasing the musicians. Even though some mistakes can be repaired though editing waveforms, many cannot. Solo each section and make sure that the "feel" of the track fits with the other parts.

Experiment with writing notation patterns or rhythmic patterns with each part. In popular music, individual parts that have a definite pattern tend to make the overall groove sound better. Not all compositions lend themselves to this approach, but many popular contemporary styles do. For example, if the chord pattern is C major, F major, G major and the pattern keeps repeating, instead of the bass player merely outlining the chords at random, each time the pattern is repeated, she would play four eighth notes, a quarter note, and a rest on the fourth beat and keep on repeating that rhythm pattern but adjusting the notes to fit each chord. Example 4 shows a bass pattern.

Example 4

Even if the parts do not lend themselves to this technique, creating symmetry within the parts results in a better arrangement. It is the same approach that is taken when composing. Composition has to have form, or there is chaos; it is the same for arranging.

The procedure described for writing patterns applies to live drumming or drum programming. Drums are always the basic foundation of the rhythm section. If the drummer does not create a solid groove, the rhythm section will never feel right. This is accomplished by playing repeated patterns that are interrupted with interesting fills—this approach keeps the part from becoming monotonous.

One of the techniques that helps avoid monotony is to change the pattern between sections. For example, if the bridge has a different pattern (than the main groove of the track) and the bridge is repeated a second time, repeat the same bridge pattern that was used in bridge number one and then return to the original pattern; the goal is to create symmetry.

> One tool used by the author (when dealing with popular music grooves) is to write numerous one- or two-bar drum and percussion patterns that sound good when played simultaneously. After laying them into the track, start eliminating individual instruments and individual patterns to create variety while not losing the feel. This helps to eliminate a boring drum or percussion part. There is a fine line between a drum part that has a groove and one that is monotonous.

Apply the same concept of rhythmic grooves when adding percussion. Create repeated patterns and keep the parts simple. The percussionist or programmer can become inventive when creating fills, but not when establishing the basic groove. Creating a good feel is the objective (not necessarily showcasing technique) when working in popular music.

The listener might think that the percussion sounds complex, but what he really is experiencing is a combination of parts. When several parts are played simultaneously, it creates rhythmic syncopation. The individual parts are not necessarily complicated.

> One of the advantages of using a computer-based recording program is being able to view the waveforms and ensure that all of the parts are aligned properly.
> As previously stated, listen to each section individually and then listen to several parts simultaneously; each part should fit just like a puzzle. If something does not feel right, experiment with moving the waveform until it gels with the other parts.

Since analog synthesis is frequently used in popular music, the arranger must think in terms of frequency range in order to place the parts properly within the arrangement. Mentally envision each part as an acoustic instrument. For example, a high part might take the place of a flute, while a mellow midrange sound might play the part of a French horn.

Since analog synthesis is usually combined with either realistic samples or acoustic instruments, the programmer must be concerned with the potential physical problems that can occur with a mixture of sonorities. The overtones heard in synthesis can sometimes be more complex than those of acoustic instruments and can create either a muddled or an unpleasant sound when heard with other parts. It is the same concern that an orchestrator has when deciding which instrumental combinations will be the most effectual within sections of an orchestration. Each time an analog sound is created, it must be considered a new instrument and treated that way.

THE ORCHESTRA AND BAND

The traditional orchestra is divided into four basic sections: strings, woodwinds, brass, and percussion. The modern popular orchestra contains synthesizers, flügelhorns, saxophones, trumpets with effects, electric guitars with effects, synthesized drums, and electric drums, along with an array of other instruments and effects.

> All popular touring bands have an engineer who controls their live sound. When using electric instruments with acoustic instruments, it is crucial that the sound engineer be familiar with what the proper balance should be. Any electric instrument can obliterate the sound of a band or orchestra. The objective is to re-create the sound on their recordings during a live performance. Sound systems are so sophisticated that they can come remarkably close with proper engineering.
> The same theory of balance applies to the mixing process in the recording studio. It is more easily achieved in the studio because of the control over the mixing environment. Automation gives the engineer and the producer total control over the soundscape.

Keyboards

Keyboard is a relatively new type of instrument. Before the invention and general use of synthesizers, a keyboardist played acoustic piano, electric piano, and/or organ. Today, *keyboard* is a general term for any instrument that has a keyboard: synthesizer, piano, organ, and so on.

The keyboard synthesizer contains all of the editing parameters in one unit. Keyboards called workstations, or MIDI controllers, are trigger rack-mounted synthesizers that do not have keyboards but contain the same sounds and editing parameters as the devices that have keyboards. (Most workstations do not contain sounds but can control a variety of devices simultaneously. This adds to the creative process, because combining synthesizers to create inventive sounds expands the composer's sound palette. A synthesizer keyboard can also act as a controller.)

> Rack-mounted versions generate the same sounds as the keyboard versions of the same instrument. They are called rack-mounted because they can be housed in a rack that can hold numerous devices. The advantage of rack-mounted sound modules is that they save a great deal of space and make it easier for the performer to generate sounds from a multitude of devices simultaneously. One keyboard can control many rack-mounted devices.

Some programmers bounce combined sounds onto one track of audio. For instance, they might use a combination of three sounds to create a smooth background (a bed). Creating a combined track allows the programmer to use the same synthesizers to create other sounds.

If a programmer uses digital audio in creative ways, several synthesizers are all that is needed to create almost any sound. The programmer should know the capabilities of a device before purchasing it. If the budget allows for a few synthesizers, a variety of sounds should be the main criterion.

Arranging for Keyboards

Keyboards are used in various ways: accompanying other instruments, playing samples of real instruments, solos, and extensively to create effects and mellow analog sounds, such as pads or beds (held chords that create a smooth background). Most synthesizers are equipped with adjustable sound parameters and effects like reverbs, delays, filters, and oscillators, which can be edited to change the sounds. For example, a vocal track can be completely altered by putting the vocal through a synthesizer and adjusting the parameters. This is generally called a vocoder; not all synthesizers have one.

The numerous uses of keyboards are left up to the arranger and the player. Because programming keyboards is complicated, it behooves the arranger to consult with the player as to the various sounds and effects that can be created. If something special is required, it is best for the arranger to contact the keyboard player prior to the session, since programming can be time consuming and the sounds should be created before the session.

> The traditional piano part (in popular music) is usually notated using a combination of chord symbols and parts. If the arranger writes a specific pattern, it will be notated where it begins and followed by chord symbols and the word *simile* (meaning similar); this means to improvise using a similar pattern.

The following are descriptions of some popular keyboards:

Electric pianos. Rhodes and Wurlitzer are the most popular brands of electric pianos. Both keyboards can be edited to change sounds. The most noticeable feature of electric pianos is the vibrato. When recorded in stereo, the electric piano creates a soothing bed.

Electric pianos combined with a variety of other sounds can make interesting sonorities. One of the most popular sounds comes from combining an electric piano and an acoustic piano playing the same part. It sounds both rich and smooth. Another effective combination is electric piano and strings, which can sound beautiful and mellow. Experimenting with other combinations can create interesting and unique sounds.

Synthesized electric pianos. Most synthesizers and samplers include a number of electric piano samples in the general MIDI patches that are included with most instruments. An infinite number of variations and combinations can be achieved through editing. Numerous edited versions of the Rhodes and Wurlitzer and less popular electric pianos are available as samples.

Most programmers who work for synthesizer manufacturers begin with a basic electric piano sound and then proceed to perform a variety of edits, which creates new sounds. Each edited version is given a new name and listed separately. One piano might sound mellow, while another will sound bell-like. Having a variety of electric piano sounds to choose from saves time for the average keyboard player.

Many performers carry out additional edits and customize and save their own sounds. Most professional musicians do this in order to offer a unique sound palette to their employer. When dealing in the competitive world of commercial music, all performers and arrangers try to present something that is unique.

Analog sounds. Sounds programmed on analog synthesizers that cannot be made by conventional instruments are generally called analog sounds. Most analog and digital synthesizers contain analog sounds in the general MIDI patches that are included with most synthesizers and samplers. An infinite number of variations and combinations can be edited to create an unlimited number of sounds. The sampled analog sounds cannot be edited in exactly the same manner as on an analog synthesizer, even though the editing parameters are similar. Analog synthesis was the original format of synthetic music. For a time, not many new analog synthesizers were being developed, but some manufacturers continue to make analog modeling synthesizers, for example, Virus B and Nord. The sounds are still popular in all forms of commercial music.

Acoustic pianos. Yamaha, Baldwin, Bösendorfer, and Steinway pianos all have different sounds. Yamaha is the most used acoustic piano in popular music, because it has a cutting sound when recorded. This said, all pianos have individual sounds, and therefore, choosing a piano becomes a matter of taste.

Synthesized acoustic pianos. Most synthesizers and samplers include a number of acoustic piano samples in the general MIDI patches that are included with most instruments. An infinite number of variations and combinations can be achieved through editing. Some of the samples tend to sound thin and percussive, whereas others are quite realistic. Combining an acoustic piano with a string-like mellow analog sound results in a very pleasing sound and can have many applications. If using this combination, be sure to have two sounds on separate faders, so that the balance can be adjusted.

Digital samples are samples of real acoustic and electric instruments, for example, acoustic guitars, drums, percussion, strings. The samples are played on a keyboard and emulate the real instruments. The quality of the samples varies greatly between manufacturers. Since purchasing sounds can be costly, listen to the sample CD or to the samples usually available for listening on the manufacturer's website.

Organs. The Hammond B3 organ, with a Leslie speaker, has been the standard organ used in all forms of popular music. There are also small reproductions of the original organ available for purchase. In fact there are virtual synthesizer software replicas of many organs, including the Hammond, that look and can be edited almost exactly like the hardware versions. (There are virtual versions of many synthesizers.) Other organs might be more appropriate for some arrangements. An infinite number of sounds can be achieved through editing.

Synthesized organs. Most synthesizers and samplers include a number of organ samples in their general MIDI patches. An infinite number of variations and combinations can be achieved through editing. (Combining an organ sound one octave above the bass can be very effective in certain styles of music, for example, club music.)

Effects generated by keyboards. Keyboards can be used to trigger MIDI effects. For example, each time a keyboard is struck, a delay occurs on the vocal track. The track is sent to a parameter in the synthesizer, which generates this effect. Almost any parameter can be MIDIed.

Guitars

Electric Guitar

The electric guitar is one of the most popular rhythm and solo instruments in popular music. It has line level outputs that route the signal either through a direct box (converts the signal for optimum signal input into the console) or directly into the recording console, an amplifier, or to both simultaneously. (All recording consoles have line level inputs.) A combination of direct and live sounds gives the engineer/producer a choice and offers a safety factor; if one signal is not usable, the other might be.

Because technology provides so many options, some engineers always want to have at least one clean signal that can be effected during the mixing process. If an effect is recorded on the same track as the original signal, there is no way to change it without rerecording the guitar.

Many rhythm sections have both a lead and a rhythm player. It is a common practice to double the rhythm guitar part when recording. This provides a wider, fuller sound when desired.

Rhythmic strumming is an integral part of the rhythm section. Most commercial guitar players consider themselves either rhythm players or lead players. In the same manner that the drummer and bass player have to sound like one unit, the rhythm guitar player has to join the drummer and bass player and lock into the groove.

As in any other style of music, rhythm guitar players specialize in playing styles. Some are good R & B players, while others are good rock or jazz players. Their styles differ and so do their choices of instruments. Some manufacturers make guitars that sound better for rock and roll, while others make guitars that sound superior for jazz, and so on. Very few guitarists play multiple styles well. Most accomplished studio musicians can cover a number of styles adequately, but it is usually prudent to hire a specialist.

Guitar solos have always been a staple in all styles of popular music. Lead guitar players are similar to lead singers—the good ones have their own "voice" (individuality). Each genre of popular music has certain characteristics that define its style. This includes the kind of solos that typify the style. Rock and roll players generally use distortion, whereas traditional jazz players have a clean, undistorted sound. Other genres have unique characteristics as well. Guitar solos generally have certain musical elements that define the style of the genre, just as the characteristics of a violin solo from the Classical period would be different from a violin solo from the Baroque period. The violinist is expected to know the "unwritten feel," characteristics and ornamentations of the specific period; the same goes for players of popular music.

Within each genre there are subgenres. As previously stated, if a guitarist is instructed to play a jazz solo, does that mean jazz from the 1940s or the 1960s, or another time period? Be specific when writing an arrangement and hire a specialist.

There are many styles of electric guitars. Solid body and hollowed body electric guitars have different sounds, and each brand has a distinct sound. Fender Stratocaster guitars and Les Paul guitars, for example, are among the most popular brands. Guitars are manufactured with a variety of pickups, which affect the sound. Arrangers must become familiar with the different sounds, since the choice of guitar will affect the sound of the overall arrangement.

There are an infinite number of effects that can be applied to the basic guitar sound. Studio players bring effects racks to recording sessions, and producers and arrangers usually experiment to find the most suitable sound for the track. Most effects can be edited and, therefore, offer the player numerous choices.

Strumming with a pick and finger picking are the most common ways of producing a sound. The metal finger slide, held by a finger of the left hand (by right-handed players), slides across the frets to produce a unique sound, similar to that made by a pedal steel guitar. Some guitars have a lever that, when lowered or raised, results in smooth pitch changing not unlike using portamento on a synthesizer.

Amplifiers also make a difference in the sound. Jazz players use different amplifiers than rock players, and so on. Distortion is the most prevalent guitar sound in rock and roll, while a clean sound is the most popular sound used by jazz guitar players. There are many brands of amplifiers, and each brand produces a distinct sound. It is important to know the differences in sound so the proper amplifier can be rented for the session.

Most engineers prefer to "take the guitar direct" (into the console) rather than miking an amplifier. The guitar is plugged directly into the recording console and bused to a track. Since guitar effects can simulate almost any kind of amplified sound, there is no need to use an amp most of the time. Most rock and roll bands prefer to use amplifiers in the studio in order to capture their live sound. Some engineers simultaneously record a direct sound and a live sound and then mix the two sounds together. This technique is customary when acoustic guitars are recorded.

Acoustic Guitar

Acoustic guitars have either nylon or steel strings. The playing style is the same as for the electric guitar, except that finger picking is used more often with acoustic guitars. The sound is usually pure and not effected in the same manner as that of an electric guitar. Reverb is generally added to make the instrument sound live.

Some acoustic guitars are made with microphone pickups. The cable is plugged into the recording console, and the signal is recorded directly in the same manner as with an electric guitar. Some engineers mix a direct signal with a live microphone signal to arrive at the final sound. Some players and engineers like the room sound to be included in the overall ambience of the sound.

Notation. Most popular music guitar parts are written with chord symbols and rhythmic indications within each bar; the rhythm notation indicates where to change the chords. Specific parts are written out. Arrangers will indicate if the part should be arpeggiated, strummed, or plucked.

Guitar players (in popular music) are hired because of the individuality that includes their feel for the style of music, their sense of time, and their technical ability and musicality. (Some guitar players specialize in either acoustic or electric guitar.)

Register. Music for the electric and acoustic guitar is written in the treble clef and sounds one octave below where it is written. The guitar is a nontransposing instrument built in C. The names of the strings are E, written below the treble clef, then A above it, D, G, B, and E on the top space. See example 5.

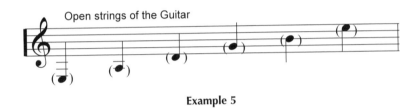

Example 5

Banjo, pedal steel, mandolin, lute, ukulele, and other stringed guitar-like instruments are used in various genres of music. Almost all world music cultures have stringed instruments. The sounds of the various guitar-like instruments can be a welcome addition to a track in conjunction with a traditional guitar part.

Basses

The bass (a.k.a. contrabass or double bass) is a unique instrument in popular music because it is used in two completely different ways: 1) as a part of the rhythm section and 2) as the low end of the string section. Some orchestral arrangements contain two distinct parts: an electric or acoustic bass playing with the rhythm section and the double basses playing with the string section.

Since the bass is an important part of an arrangement, particular attention has to be paid to the intrinsic role it plays not only in sonority but also in creating rhythm. In popular music, the bass player and the drummer must work as a unit. If they do not work well together, there will be no groove. When bass and drums are programmed, the bass drum and the bass will sometimes play exactly the same rhythm pattern. What occurs is a very deep rhythm combination that creates the feel of the track.

In a traditional symphonic setting, the double basses usually read the same notes as the celli, but they sound one octave lower. They create a deep, resonant sound. In popular music, the bass helps to create a foundation for the rhythm section by playing rhythmic patterns that usually form an inseparable combination with the drums. In all forms of popular music, the use of the bass continues to evolve.

The arranger has to be concerned that the low frequencies of the two parts, playing simultaneously, do not become muddy. It could be a problem if the notes for the electric rhythm bass were written in the same range as those for the double basses. The parts have to be written with this in mind.

Contrabass

A contrabass, also called a double bass, is pitched an octave below the basses (celli are technically considered the basses) and is the instrument most commonly used in a symphony orchestra.

Electric Bass

Electric basses are used in almost all forms of contemporary music. Some players specialize in rock and roll, while others only play jazz. (Not all jazz electric bass players play upright acoustic bass.)

Synthesized Bass

Synthesized basses are extensively used on recordings and in live performances. Some arrangers use several synthesized bass parts, with different sounds, within one arrangement. When a synthesized bass is programmed, there are an infinite number of usable sounds. Editing filters, oscillators, and effects help to create almost any sound that comes to the programmer's imagination. The arranger must be aware of the trends in popular bass sounds. This information will be valuable in choosing a bass sound for the assignment. Not only do certain sounds become trends in popular music, but certain kinds of rhythmic patterns also prevail. This generally evolves because a producer will hear a hit record that has a distinct bass pattern and emulate it for her next record. Then the domino effect occurs, and soon similar patterns are frequently heard on commercials and records. Commercial arrangers must be aware of trends, because it is common to receive an assignment to emulate a current style.

There are primarily two kinds of electric bass: one has four strings (the standard), and the other has six strings (rare). Several custom-made electric basses have five strings, the lowest note being a C (below the bass clef) rather than an E (below the bass clef) found on four-string acoustic basses.

Notation. Bass parts, in popular music, are usually written with chord symbols above the notes, so the player can improvise around the written part. Orchestral contrabass parts are always written.

Bass players (in popular music) are hired because of their individuality, which includes their feel for the style of music, their sense of time, their technical ability, and their musicality. Most studio bass players can read music and therefore will work quickly to achieve the overall performance expected by the arranger. Commercials are recorded in short recording sessions, so the performers have to work quickly and accurately. These are the traits inherent in the best studio performers.

Register for the four-string bass. The bass sounds one octave below the written pitch and is written in the bass clef. The open strings are the written notes: E written on the first ledger line below the bass clef, the A above it, the D above the A, and the G above the D. See example 6.

Example 6

Register for the six-string electric bass. The six-string electric bass is not commonly used, is tuned the same as a guitar, is written in the treble clef, and sounds an octave lower than written. The lowest written note is E, below the third ledger line below middle C; the following notes are (written above the E) A, D, G, B, and E. See example 7.

Example 7

Drums

The drummer, in popular music, is the backbone of the rhythm section; she creates the basic groove. In orchestral music, drums (percussion in an orchestral context) contribute rhythm, effects, and colors to the orchestration.

The traditional acoustic drum set (used in popular music) is made up of many individual percussive instruments, which are referred to as a drum kit or trap drums. Most kits are played with various styles of drumsticks, brushes, and different sized mallets (used mainly for cymbals and tom-toms); each creates a unique sound. In popular music, drummers are hired for their individuality, feel, and technique. The average drum kit consists of:

1. Snare drum,
2. Bass drum (also called a kick drum),
3. Hi-hat cymbals, which open and close with a foot pedal,
4. Crash cymbals (used for accents),
5. Ride cymbal (has an open, ringing sound, and is used for rhythm patterns),
6. A variety of other cymbals,
7. Large and small tom-toms, and
8. Some drummers also mix in electric drums, which can either be triggered by an attachment that is connected to an acoustic drum or by directly striking a pad, which produces various programmable electric drum sounds.

Register

Drum parts are written in the bass clef, with the lowest space indicating the bass drum, the third space from the bottom indicating the snare drum, Xs above the top line indicating the hi-hat, and other spaces indicating tom-toms, which are usually marked "tom-toms" above the notes; other cymbals are usually marked with the name of the instrument next to the note. See example 8.

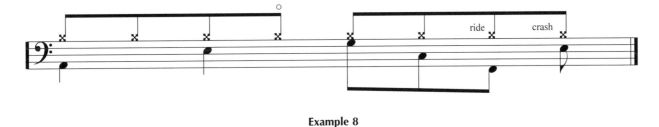

Example 8

An acoustic drum part can be recorded and then used as a triggering device to generate electric drum samples that can either replace the original part or be played simultaneously with the original part. This is quite common in country music.

Since the groove is of utmost importance in popular music, it is crucial that the arranger be aware of current trends, in both rhythmic grooves and sounds. Some genres of music, such as rock, primarily use a live drummer; some genres, such as hip-hop, primarily use drum programmers. Many tracks include a combination of a live drummer and synthesized drums and percussion.

It is not unusual for arrangers or music producers to record live drums onto analog tape and transfer them to a computer audio program (e.g., Pro-Tools or Digital Performer) for editing, because they like the warm sound of analog tape as opposed to digital hard disk recording.

Many people like the sound of analog recording because they think that it sounds warmer and more pleasing than digital. Some engineers feel that transferring the analog tracks to digital audio defeats the purpose, because the sound changes. It ultimately boils down to personal preference.

The advantage of transferring tape to a digital computer program is the ability to manipulate and edit the sounds, using a fast, nondestructive process. This enables the music producers to present numerous variations and make changes quickly. They can always revert to the original program, because even though the program can be edited many times, the original waveforms are never erased.

The same recording process is used for percussion, for example, congas, bongos, shakers, and tambourines. Many arrangers create synthesized percussion sounds by editing and adding to existing sounds. These sounds are not an attempt to duplicate the sound of real instruments, but are rather an attempt to create new sounds that achieve the same rhythmic result as traditional percussion instruments do.

> Synthesizer manufacturers make *dedicated* (contains only drum sounds) drum machines, some of which contain hundreds of sounds that can be edited to achieve a unique quality. Third-party manufacturers also sell myriad sounds. Some drum machines have very sophisticated editing parameters and allow the programmer great creativity. This is also true of drum machines that are virtual (software) versions.
>
> Professional drum programmers spend endless hours creating and editing drum and percussive sounds. It is their "feel" along with their individual pallet of sounds that makes them unique.

Drummers, percussionists, and drum programmers (in popular music) are hired because of their individuality, which includes their feel for the style of music, their sense of time, and their technical ability.

Timpani

Timpani (also called kettledrums) are standard in symphony orchestras as well as in popular music orchestras. They are usually made of copper and are covered with a skin.

If not overused, the sound of timpani can make a distinct statement within the arrangement. There is nothing else in the orchestra that produces that deep, percussive sound. When combined with the basses, a rich low end is created. Timpani are played with mallets.

Register. There are four basic timpani drums, parts for which are written in the bass clef. Their tones are adjusted through the use of a foot pedal—the lower the pedal is pushed, the higher the tone.

The lowest drum goes from C, two ledger lines below the clef, to G, on the first ledger line; the second drum goes from F to C, the third drum from B-flat to F, and the fourth drum from E-flat to A-flat, all above the lowest C. See example 9.

Example 9

Timpani are popular in hip-hop music, because the power of the low end is so effective.

Percussion Instruments

A percussion instrument is defined as something that is struck or shaken; it can be made out of wood, metal, skin, or numerous other materials. Some percussion instruments have a traditional tone, and some do not. Many sampled and analog percussion sounds are included in both software and hardware drum machines, and general MIDI patches are included with most synthesizers. Most drum programmers consider percussion as a part of the overall drum program and therefore program percussion simultaneously with the traditional drums.

In popular music, percussion plays a major role in both the feel and sonority of the arrangement. The percussion is an intrinsic member of the rhythm section and should be scrutinized to make certain that the parts fit into the overall rhythmic puzzle.

Piano

The sound of the piano is made when the player's hands depress the keys, which in turn trigger wooden hammers that hit the strings. Most full pianos have eighty-eight keys. (The Bösendorfer piano [made in Austria] has an extra range—down to F0—and has ninety-two keys.)

The sound of the piano can be applied in several ways: as a solo instrument, to accompany other instruments or singers, and as tonal colors. It is the most versatile instrument.

> Most pianists specialize in a style, e.g., classical, jazz, country, pop, rock, R&B, and so on. In all forms of popular music, the most important element of a performer's playing is being true to the style of the genre. For example, most rhythm and blues players have their roots in gospel music and have played in the church; therefore they have a traditional background and feel for R&B that emanates from gospel music. Most country music performers grew up in the southern United States, where country music is popular; they learned the roots of the music. The same goes for the traditions of jazz and other music genres.

Range. The range of the piano is from A (8va basso) below the bass clef to C (2va) above the treble clef.

Celesta

The celesta has a small keyboard with soft hammers that hit metal bars, creating a bell-like sound, which is very pretty and soothing. The sound is most effective in creating colors and should not be overused. Melodic celesta passages, in combination with other instruments, like the flute, create a sparkling sound. Arpeggiated passages and chords are also effective when used sparsely.

Range. The celesta is written from C in the bass clef to C two octaves above the treble clef. The celeste sounds one octave above where it is written. See example 10.

Example 10

Percussive Instruments Played with Mallets

Vibraphone

For many years, the vibraphone (vibes) has been a popular instrument in jazz; the texture has also been used extensively in film scores. The vibraphone is electric and has metal bars and a pedal that sustains the notes when depressed; there is a control switch that generates vibrato at various speeds. The notes are arranged like those for a piano.

Normally, the vibraphone is played using two mallets, but parts can be written for three and four mallets; mallets can be hard or soft, depending on the sound desired. When using more than two mallets, the player needs time to manipulate them, and this must be taken into consideration when writing the part; the tempo cannot be too fast. Vibes parts are often written as a combination with the piano.

Range. The vibraphone is a nontransposing instrument written in the treble clef. It has a range from F directly below middle C to F, the fourth space above the treble clef. Vibraphones are made in different sizes and ranges. See example 11.

Example 11

Xylophone

The xylophone is one of many instruments that have wooden bars. The bars are struck, most often, with wooden hammer-like mallets. The xylophone is played in a manner similar to that of the vibraphone, except that the xylophone has no sustain pedal. The notes are arranged like those for a piano. Used sparingly, the distinct wooden sound is effective when combined with orchestral instruments. Xylophones are manufactured in different sizes and their ranges vary.

   Range. Notes for the xylophone are written in the treble clef and sound one octave higher than written. The lowest note sounds an F, the first space on the treble clef, and the highest note is C, one octave above the second line C above the treble clef. See example 12.

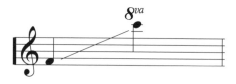

Example 12

Marimba

The marimba is similar to a xylophone and is struck with hard or soft hammer-like mallets. Notes for the marimba are written in the treble clef and sound where they are written. Like the xylophone, the marimba has wooden bars and no sustain pedal, and the bars are arranged like a piano keyboard. The marimba has a mellower sound than the xylophone.

   Range. The range is from F below middle C to C, one octave above the second line C of the treble clef. Marimbas come in different sizes and their ranges vary. The bass marimba is very popular because it has a deep wooden sound that cannot be duplicated by any other instrument. See example 13.

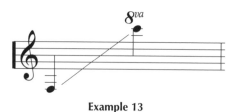

Example 13

Balaphones are from the African countries, and their tunings and number of wooden bars vary from country to country; they are struck with various mallets. Their unique sound, used sparingly, is very effective.

Glockenspiel

The glockenspiel (bells) is a small instrument, consisting of two rows of graduated metal bars with no sustain pedal that is played with two small wooden, soft mallets or brass mallets. It has a bell-like quality and is affective in combination with other instruments. Parts are written in the treble clef and sound two octaves above where they are written.

   Range. The lowest written note is G below middle C, and the highest written note is C, two octaves above middle C. See example 14.

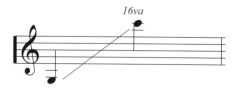

Example 14

Even though the instrument can be played at a rapid pace, because the bells ring, the natural reverberation can create a cloudy sound. This must be taken into consideration when writing the part. It is an instrument that must be used sparingly, or the effect will not be appreciated.

Chimes

Chimes are long metal tubes that are hung vertically and played like a piano keyboard. The chimes are hit with wooden hammers and sound much like church bells. The sound must not be overused.

Range. The range is from middle C on the treble clef to F on the top line of the clef. Chimes sound one octave above the written notes. See example 15.

Example 15

Latin Percussion

The most popular Latin percussive instruments are the conga drums, bongo drums, cowbells, go-go bells, and all forms of shakers, guiro, timbales, claves, and maracas. Most Latin percussion originated in Africa. Afro-Cuban music developed from the rhythms of Africa.

If an assignment calls for a specific Latin style, hire players who are familiar with the music of that country. Each country has its own rhythms, instruments, and traditions. Hiring a Cuban percussionist to play on a Mexican track would be analogous to a rock and roll guitar player being hired to play a jazz solo.

In popular music, percussion players specialize in percussion and are usually not traditional drummers who play drum kits or mallets. Orchestral percussion players generally are trained to play all of the instruments.

There is an abundance of percussive instruments from almost every country in the world. We will concentrate on the most popular instruments.

Congas. Most conga players use two drums: a high-pitched drum and a low-pitched drum. Some use three or four drums, each with a different tuning. Tightening or loosening the drumheads tunes the drums. They are generally played with the hands.

Congas have been a staple in both Latin and popular music for many years. A well-played conga part fits perfectly with the rest of the rhythm section.

In Caribbean Latin music, there are a variety of percussive instruments, each playing a traditional style. The percussion section must work as a unit. Latin conga players have the ability to lay down a solid foundation for the percussion section to work with. They also possess an excellent sense of time and technique.

> Some conga players and percussionists specialize in playing rhythm and blues. It is a unique style of playing that has been borrowed from the traditional Latin techniques.

Bongo drums are essentially high-pitched conga drums. Bongos are assembled as two drums, which are held together with metal. Each drum can be tuned individually. Bongos played along with congas make a good combination.

Bata drums are similar to conga drums. *Oconcolo* is the small drum, *itotele* is the medium-sized drum, and the iya is the large drum. They are tunable, and many use buffalo hides for the head of the drums. Batas are played in the same manner as conga drums.

Cowbells (taken from bells worn on cows' necks) are made of metal and played with a small stick. They are essential to the Caribbean-Latin rhythm section. It is traditional to play syncopated rhythms that help to form the rhythmic foundation of the groove.

Go-go bells are essentially high-pitched cowbells and are played in the same manner as cowbells.

Shakers come in all sizes and shapes and are usually made of gourds (a hard-skinned fruit) filled with a substance, such as beans or rice, that can be shaken in time with the groove. Maracas are an example of shakers.

A cabaza is shaker-like; it is round and has a handle and metal strips around it, which are struck by moving the metal against the opposite hand. The effect is the same as that achieved with a shaker, but it sounds more metallic.

A tambourine is a single- or double-headed drum with small metal cymbal-like pieces surrounding the head. It is played by shaking or striking the head with one's hand. The tambourine is widely used in popular music as well as in Latin music.

The claves are two short thick pieces of wood that are hit together to produce a rhythm pattern. Claves are also used in popular music.

Most Latin percussion players do not read music and are hired for their unique feel. If more than one player is being hired, it is wise to hire people who have worked together; they will play better as a unit.

THE STRING SECTION

The string section, made up of violins, violas, celli, and basses, is the backbone of the symphony orchestra. Its capability of playing rapid passages, of sounding equally pleasing when played *ppp* (very softly) or *fff* (extremely loud), and the beautiful blend of the instruments make the string section unique. The strings accomplish many functions within an arrangement. Close harmonies written in the middle to lower registers produce warm-sounding beds; high unison violins can sail on top of an arrangement, while celli and violas play unison lines, gliding through the baritone range, which forms rich and full-sounding inner parts. Almost any emotion can be generated with a well-crafted string arrangement. Solo instruments, such as a solo violin or cello, can add contrast and beauty to the traditional sectional sonorities.

Strings adapt to many successful combinations with other instruments. Combining French horns with violas, bassoons with celli, tubas with basses, and flutes and oboes with violins fashions complementary sonorities. An adventuresome arranger experiments with unusual combinations.

> Professional string players can play almost anything that comes to the composer's imagination. Try all ideas and then make adjustments. It is important for the arranger to understand the fingering and positions on the string instruments in order to write for them.

The string instruments are nontransposing instruments that sound where they are written, with the exception of the double bass, which sounds one octave below where it is written.

There is an extensive repertoire for violins and celli in all genres. Violas and double basses are not popular solo instruments in the classical repertoire.

Double, triple, and quadruple stops, which are notated with brackets around them, can be played on all of the stringed instruments. The arranger must be familiar with how long it takes the player to move from one position to another. Make sure that two notes are not on the same string or the chord can obviously not be played. Double stops can be sustained, but triple and quadruple stops cannot be sustained, because it is impossible for the bow to hit all of the strings simultaneously; these stops are either plucked or bowed. If you have any doubts about what can be played, consult with a string player.

The student must learn the various bowing techniques and technical limitations of the stringed instruments, or his ability to write for strings will be greatly limited. It is impossible to achieve the variety of sounds that is available with a live string section on synthesizers, because of the bowing techniques and the missing feel of live musicians.

Bowing techniques are an integral part of the sound of the string section. The main techniques are:

1. **Arco** means to play with a bow; e.g., after a pizzicato passage (plucked), the score is marked arco, which means the player resumes playing with a bow.
2. **Pizzicato** means to pluck the strings; the effect is extensively used and is a sound unique to strings.
3. **Up-bow** means the player moves the bow upward, as opposed to **down-bow**, where the player moves the bow down. Each technique creates a different sound.
4. A **slur** marking is a line that connects a series of notes and indicates that the player should play those notes with one stroke of the bow. This creates a smooth-sounding passage. If there are no slurs indicated, the player will alternate between up-bow and down-bow movements.

5. A **staccato** marking, which looks like a period symbol placed above or below the notes, indicates alternating up- and down-bows played quickly. **Spiccato** has the same symbol as staccato, but the bow bounces on the strings; the word *spiccato* should be indicated on the score to differentiate it from the staccato bowing technique. **Jete** has the same symbol that indicates a bouncing effect, except in this case, bowing markings are included that indicate how long the bow should stay in the same direction.

6. **Detache** (meaning detached) is marked with a line under each note; the bow must move quickly through the note and remain on the note for the length of the note. Detache is normally used with dynamics that are not too soft, and the note values and tempo must give the player enough time to perform the bowing; if the notes change too quickly, the bowing cannot be performed.

7. **Loure** has the same marking as detache, except it contains slur markings, which indicate that a series of notes should be played during one bowing direction, with a brief stop between attacks, and each time there is a new slur, the direction of the bow changes.

8. **Tremolo** is the bow moving rapidly through a certain note value without regard to tempo. It creates a dramatic effect and is effective played *p* or *fff*. The marking is a series of lines under a note(s).

9. **Sul ponticello** means to play close to the bridge. This creates a very thin sound and works well while playing a tremolo.

10. **Sul tasto** means to play near or over the fingerboard. This creates a nondescript tone.

11. **Col legno** (meaning "with the wood") is achieved by hitting the strings with the wood of the bow; this also creates a dramatic effect and is most effectively used in small staccato sections. The word *normal* is marked as an indication that the player should return to normal bowing.

12. **Portamento** is a sliding of the finger from one note to another and can only be achieved by the string section in an orchestra. (Portamento is very popular in synthesizer programming.) This is marked with a line connecting the high to the low note.

13. A **mute,** which is normally a piece of wood, is inserted on the bridge, creating a mellow, muffled sound. The part is marked **sordini** to indicate the use of mutes and **senza sordini** to indicate no mutes.

14. **Sur la touché** means that the bow is played higher up on the fingerboard than the bridge; this creates a pure and softer sound.

15. **Vibrato** is the signature sound of all string players. It is a rapid movement of the finger below the pitch but returning quickly. Vibrato is a technique that is developed by each player and one of the main factors that determines individuality. In early music, vibrato was frowned upon, but later it became an accepted technique. If the composer does not want vibrato, it is marked in the score by *no vibrato* or *N.V.*

16. A **trill** is a rapid movement of the finger from one note to another. It is marked in the score with the symbol *tr* and sometimes has the secondary note indicated in parentheses; if there is no note indicated, the common practice is to trill between the written note and a note one half or a full step higher.

17. **Harmonics** (the overtones that are heard when a note is played) can be played as individual tones on stringed instruments. This creates a light and glittering effect. Harmonics can be played in two ways on the violin: 1) **natural harmonics**, which are played on the open strings by lightly placing a finger a perfect fourth above the open string, resulting in a harmonic that sounds two octaves above the sound of the open string, and 2) **artificial harmonics**, which are played by placing a finger a perfect fourth above a stopped finger (a finger placed on a string to create a specific note). In this case, the harmonic sounds two octaves above the stopped note—not the fourth. For example, if the desired note is two octaves above the open G string, the finger is placed lightly on middle C. Harmonics are notated by placing a small, diamond-shaped note a fourth above the basic note.

We have just discussed the most commonly used bowing techniques; there are additional bowings.

Violin

The violin is played by drawing a bow across the strings, plucking the strings (pizzicato), or striking the strings in a percussive manner. The violinist places his fingers in different places (called positions) on the fingerboard. Practically, there are eight positions, but they can go as high as fifteen.

Register. The violin, written in the treble clef, has four open strings, which are tuned in perfect fifths. The lowest string is G below middle C, followed by D above middle C, A above middle C, and E on the top space of the treble clef. See example 16.

Example 16

The orchestral violin section is divided into two sections: first and second violins. The concertmaster of the orchestra has traditionally been the first violinist.

Viola

The viola is played in exactly the same manner as the violin. The main difference is that because the viola is larger, it is more cumbersome to move rapidly through fingerings. This is a minor consideration, because well-trained violists have excellent technique.

Register. Music for the viola is written in the alto clef and has four open strings, which are tuned in perfect fifths. The strings are C, one octave below middle C, G below middle C, D above middle C, and A above middle C. See example 17.

Example 17

Cello

The celli are considered the basses of the orchestra. The cello is much larger than the viola and is played by sitting in a chair and holding the instrument between the player's legs. Because of the size of the cello, the fingering differs slighting from that of a viola, and it is more difficult to move around with the same agility and ease as one can on a viola or violin.

Register. Music for the cello is written in the bass clef. The cello has four open strings, which are the same as those on the viola but one octave lower. The notes are C two octaves below middle C, G one octave below middle C, D below middle C, and A below middle C. See example 18.

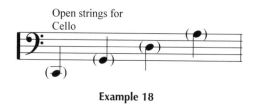

Example 18

Because of the cello's size, double stops and chords are more easily played on opening strings.

Double Bass

The double basses, in an orchestral setting, usually play the same part as the celli but sound one octave lower. The double basses are actually the subbasses of the orchestra. The celli provide the clarity in the sound when playing the same part one octave higher.

The player holds the instrument while standing or while sitting on a high stool. Because the instrument is so large and the bow relatively small, the player cannot play legato passages or hold long notes with one bow stroke. The full, rich sound of pizzicato has made the upright bass the instrument of choice in traditional jazz ensembles.

Register. The double bass, written in the bass clef, sounds one octave lower than where it is written and is tuned in fourths. The open strings are E one octave below middle C, A one octave below middle C, D below middle C, and G below middle C. (Many concert basses have a low C string.) Refer back to example 6 earlier in the chapter.

The double bass, also referred to as an acoustic bass, is rarely used in pop music but is popular in jazz. Therefore, when a budget allows for only a small number of musicians, the double bass is usually the first instrument to be eliminated.

The string section consists of instruments that can play very high (violins) to very low (double basses), which offers the arranger a wide variety of choices.

When creating an arrangement, the arranger might feel that the arrangement needs a boost, which can be accomplished by building the string arrangement. For example, the arrangement could start with low strings and then add violas followed by violins. Creative string arranging is one of the most valuable "tools" of the arranger.

In a symphony orchestra, it takes many strings to create a full, rich sound. This can be accomplished with fewer musicians in the studio by using a technique called overdubbing. This means to double or triple the parts on additional tracks. (This is not always viable because of budget restrictions.)

If the number of musicians is limited, it is advisable for the arranger not to write the violin parts too high. Without a substantial number of violinists (at least eight playing in unison) it will sound very thin in the studio. By writing in lower registers and having all members of that section playing the same part, the composer will make the section sound richer. An experienced engineer can help generate a rich sound. Using the proper microphones and knowing how to place them are a major factor in the resulting sound.

Two violas and two celli can sound rich in the studio if the part is arranged properly. The arranger should choose the instruments needed in the string section according to the budget and the needs of a particular arrangement. For example, only violins might be needed; other times, four violas and two celli will accomplish the sound. Most studio arrangers, through experience, know how to divide the sections.

Harp

The harp is an unusual instrument. It is plucked and has strings, pedals, and more than seven octaves. No other orchestral instrument can create the same sound. In an orchestral setting, the harp blends especially well with strings and woodwinds; it is also a beautiful solo instrument and a valued member of small combos.

The harp is not considered a chromatic instrument. (The orchestrator must understand the technical limitations of the instrument in order to write chromatically.) A harp can play chords, single notes, arpeggios (broken chords), and glissandos (fingers sliding across the strings). The glissando, the harp's signature sound, provides a beautiful shimmering effect. Playing a glissando (gliss), with the pitches alternating from high to low, low to high, or in random motion, is the signature sound of the harp. The harp should be used sparingly to be most effective in an orchestral setting.

Register. The modern harp is a complex instrument. It has seven pedals, one for each scale degree. Each pedal represents a note in the diatonic scale. The harp is tuned in the key of C-flat when all of the pedals are in their natural positions. When all of the pedals are depressed to the second notch, the instrument is tuned in the key of C; when the pedals are depressed to the third position, the harp is tuned in the key of C-sharp. It takes the player time to adjust the pedals, and the arranger should take this into consideration. Since the harp is complicated, the arranger should consult with the player if there are any technical questions. The arranger must be aware of the most appropriate enharmonic spellings of the notes to make it easier for the harpist to change the pedals. Most harpists mark pedal changes on their parts.

The harp is played with four fingers on each hand, and therefore the arranger should not write chords of more than four notes. Harmonics can be played and are indicated by placing a zero above the note(s). Harmonics sound one octave above the written note(s).

Synthesized Strings

There are many restrictions when programming synthesized or sampled strings. Because live string players use numerous bowing techniques and a great deal of emotion in their playing, it is very difficult to duplicate the same sound on synthesizers. There are several ways to make synthesizers or samples sound "real" on a recording.

Record the synthesizer parts and then add live players playing the same parts. The combination makes the synthesizers sound real and adds a human feel to an otherwise primarily electronic sound. The intonation, vibrato, and dynamics of the live strings bring animation to the synthesized parts. Sometimes the live strings sound full enough to eliminate the synthesized parts.

Another option is to play the lower parts on synthesizers and use live players on the violin parts. The lower parts, being less obtrusive, will sometimes sound real within this context.

Mixing real and synthesized strings together can enhance the richness of the overall sound. This requires experimentation, because the analog quality has to fit the tonality of the rest of the orchestration.

> Since there are literally thousands of samples of string sounds to choose from, the arranger must be selective when trying to achieve a synergy with live strings. If the sonorities do not match, the combination will not work.
>
> It is sometimes desirable to create an unusual sound. Choosing interesting synthesizer sounds mixed with live strings and then adding effects can achieve this.

When arranging the synthesized parts, stay within the range of the live instruments. Some synthesizers allow the programmer to play notes that are outside of the range of the real sampled instrument. This automatically creates an unrealistic sound. Write within the best-sounding range of the real instrument, which is called the tessitura. This will make the parts sound more realistic.

Playing full chords, especially in the higher octaves, tends to sound very thin and unrealistic on synthesizers. High, synthesized violins and violas sound best played in unison. The same theory should be applied to live string writing, if the violin and viola sections are small. The section will not have the same effect as a symphony orchestra that has a full complement of violins and violas.

Try not to make the synthesized strings too loud in the mix. Adding reverb and delay and keeping the parts relatively soft is an excellent disguise; this makes the overall string sound more realistic.

Try not to write complicated parts. For example, fast runs are a typical device used by arrangers with a live section; this, generally, does not work well with synthesizers. One reason for this is that many of the synthesized sounds do not "speak" quickly enough and there is a lag in the sound, which is called latency.

Most professional string programs (sounds) offer sounds with different bowing techniques (e.g., arco, staccato, etc.), dynamics (e.g., *f*, *ppp*), solo instruments, or full sections. Even though these choices help to achieve realism, they still do not sound real unless some of the techniques just discussed are employed.

STRING COMBINATIONS FOR THE STUDIO

Since it is unusual to have a budget large enough to hire a full string section for a commercial, the arranger must have options. The choice of instruments usually depends on the demands of the arrangement. Below are some suggestions:

Six first violins, five second violins, four violas, two celli, and one double bass (if needed) is a large string section for a commercial. Most of the time, the budget does not allow for this large a section.

Eight violins, two violas, and two celli will sound good in the studio, as long as the violins are not written too high. Experimentation and experience help the arranger learn which studio combinations sound best for certain types of arrangements.

Some arrangers might use only violins, violas, or celli. In the heyday of disco, almost all of the records had live violin parts. Many arrangers would only use six or eight live violins augmented by synthesizers.

> There are several nontraditional uses of strings. The fiddle (violin) has been a mainstay of country and Irish music for many years. The style is very specialized. Many fiddle players cannot read music. In this case, guide them.

The solo violin has also been popular as a jazz solo instrument. The solo cello is used in rock and roll bands as well as in pop and folk acts.

The arranger should be aware of the various styles and techniques and learn how to write in these styles.

BRASS

In popular music, brass plays many roles. In most older rhythm and blues tracks, the brass was used for accents and thematic unison melodic lines. Highlighting tracks with a surprise "blast" or long countermelodies has always been a trademark of R & B. Intricate brass and tasty ensemble parts have always been popular in traditional and commercial jazz arrangements.

Since most R & B horn sections are small, they are usually composed of brass and saxophones. A typical section would be two trumpets, one tenor saxophone, one trombone, and a baritone saxophone. To "fatten up" the sound in a recording studio, many producers double the horn parts.

The use of brass by master arranger Nelson Riddle on Frank Sinatra recordings is a fine example of how to use brass in a commercial jazz style. The availability of mutes and plungers offers the arranger an array of tonal colors to choose from.

The most popular brass instruments in popular music are trumpets, trombones, French horns, and tubas. Throughout musical history, there have been many versions of these instruments (tuned to different keys). Most modern arrangers use trumpets in B-flat, trombones in C, French horns in F, and tubas in C. There are instances when special instruments are used; e.g., the piccolo trumpet (pitched in B-flat and playing one octave above a B-flat trumpet) is popular in film scoring; sousaphones, baritone horns, and coronets are standard brass band instruments; flügelhorns are used in all styles of music.

Because of the physical energy that it takes to play a brass instrument, the arranger must take the following into consideration: 1) Do not write the parts too high or too low for long periods of time. The player cannot sustain very high or very low parts for long periods of time without faltering. The embouchure (placement of lips) can become weak, because of strain, and the player will not be able to sustain the pitches. 2) Trumpets are most effective when used sparingly.

Brass instruments have metal mouthpieces of various sizes. The player creates an embouchure (the placement of lips and tongue) and blows into the mouthpiece.

Trumpet

The trumpet is the highest of the brass instruments. The instrument has three valves. By adjusting his embouchure, the player can change the natural harmonic overtones; by pressing various combinations of the three valves, half steps are achieved. Double and triple tonguing, slurring between notes, rapid trills, and special big band playing techniques are all characteristic of the playing style.

In a large setting (i.e., big band, orchestra) there are usually four or five trumpets. Trumpets playing in octaves can be very powerful. Three- and four-part harmony produces a full and exciting sound.

Big bands always have a specialist called a lead trumpet player, who can play higher than the other players and sustain high parts for long periods of time. Normally, the second trumpet player has the role of the jazz solo player.

There are numerous concertos and chamber pieces written for trumpet. The sound of the trumpet can be altered through the use of three types of mutes:

1. The **cup mute** is the softest sounding and blends well with other sections.
2. The **straight mute** has a more cutting sound.
3. The **harmon mute** has the thinnest sound.
4. Trumpet players also use a **rubber plunger** or a plastic cup, which is held in one hand and opened and closed over the sound coming out of the bell. Sometimes the players use their hand to accomplish the same sound as a plunger.

The trumpet can be affective with the proper use of mutes. Playing a soft section using a cup mute and removing the mute and playing a fortissimo passage gives the illusion of two different instruments.

Muted trumpets with flutes, trumpets, and tenor saxophones playing in unison or in octaves, in addition to other orchestral combinations, make interesting sonorities.

Register. B-flat trumpets require a transposition of one full tone up: If the trumpet plays a D, it will sound a C. A trumpet has a range from E below middle C, to high notes above G, two octaves above middle C. The arranger has to be careful not to write high parts for a long period of time. The high notes are very difficult to play, and the players may not consistently hit the notes with the correct intonation. Trumpets sound best in their middle range. They can sound powerful playing four-part harmony or playing in octaves (two trumpets high and two low) or in unison. Do not overwrite the trumpet parts; they are more effective when used as a distinct musical color. See example 19.

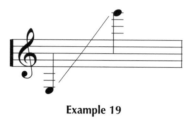

Example 19

Tenor Slide Trombone

A tenor slide trombone is a nontransposing instrument. Adjusting the player's embouchure changes the natural overtones. The slide trombone does not have valves, and therefore the chromatics are achieved by adjusting the length of the slide. Since it is difficult to move the slide quickly, fast parts should not generally be written for the trombone, although many jazz trombonists have remarkable technical ability and can play as quickly as trumpet players.

Most big bands and orchestras have three or four trombones. The bass trombone usually plays the lowest-pitched trombone part. A trombone section can sound smooth and full or loud and important like it does in a marching band. Trombones blend well with the lower strings and the French horns.

Whether arranged in harmony or unison lines, trombones have a distinct blend. The glissando is the most recognizable sound of the trombone, because of the player's ability to slide from one note to another. The arranger must study the instrument before writing a glissando, because not all notes can slide to other notes. Low, percussive pedal tones are also a common use of trombones. Some solo trombone players (e.g., Tommy Dorsey, J. J. Johnson) have amazing dexterity, considering the difficulty of the instrument.

In classical music, the trombone is not popular as a solo instrument. It is included in brass chamber music.

Range. The average range is from E two octaves below middle C, to B-flat above middle C. Some players can play higher, but the arranger should not write that high without knowing that it can be played. Trombonists use the same style mutes as trumpets. The plunger is the most recognizable, because as it enters and exits the bell, it creates an unusual "wa-wa" sound. See example 20.

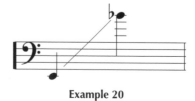

Example 20

Valve trombones exist, but they are rare. Some jazz players play valve trombones because it allows them to play faster. There is a definite difference in sound between a valve and a slide trombone. Be certain what sound you want before writing.

Note: During the Civil War, the marching bands used valve trombones with the bell facing over the player's shoulder so the troops behind them could hear them more clearly. Other brass instruments were designed in the same manner.

Bass Trombone

The bass trombone is a valuable addition to the low end of the band or orchestra. It provides a unique resonant and rich sound. No other instrument creates the same resonance when playing low notes. It is effective when playing in unison with tubas.

Range. Music for the bass trombone is written in the bass clef and has a range from F below the bass clef to middle C, or, in some cases, depending on the player, a B-flat above middle C. See example 21.

Example 21

French Horn

The modern French horn is pitched in the key of F. (Some symphony players prefer the use the horn in B-flat.) As with the other brass instruments just discussed, the player changes the natural overtones of the French horn by changing her embouchure. French horns have three valves, which enable the player to achieve chromatic tones.

The majestic sound of French horns playing in unison or in fifths cuts through an orchestra with an important and sometimes soothing sound. No other orchestral instrument can achieve the same effect. The room seems to be filled with the magnificent sound. Most orchestras have three or four French horn players.

The French horn player uses a cup mute and a straight mute; unlike trumpet players, he cannot use a harmon mute. Players usually keep one hand over the bell in order to achieve a muffled, far-off sound; he also plays with an open bell. Do not write high parts for the French horn that last a long period of time. It is difficult to play, and the sound of the horns will seem overused.

There are numerous solo French horn pieces written for orchestra and chamber music. Jazz French horn solo players are rare, but French horns are used in jazz orchestras. They blend well with every section of the orchestra. They are best used for legato passages. Staccato and sforzando are part of their signature sound. The arranger must give the players space to rest because the instrument is difficult to play and the performer's lips can easily become fatigued.

Range. The French Horn is written a perfect fifth above where it sounds. It is written in the treble clef and has a range from F, the first space below the bass clef, to between D, the fourth line on the treble clef. Some players can play higher. See example 22.

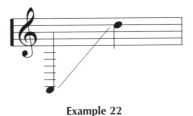

Example 22

Many arrangers do not write a key signature and mark all of the accidentals. This is the historical way of writing for the instrument. Most contemporary arrangers use key signatures.

Tuba

The modern C tuba is a nontransposing instrument, sounds where it is written, and is the lowest pitched brass instrument. (In symphony orchestras, some tubas are pitched in double B-flat or E-flat.)

The tuba and the bass trombone blend well playing in unison. The tuba adds an incredible low end to the orchestra or small group, for example, in Dixieland or band music. It also works well playing the lowest note of a trombone section. It this case, the bass trombone is usually written more like a tenor trombone part.

Tubas are pitched in various keys. Classical music makes use of these instruments. Many tubas have four or more valves, which help to achieve better intonation.

The tuba is not often used as a solo instrument. An exception is in the song "Tubby the Tuba," a very popular children's piece written by George Kleinsinger for symphony orchestra. Jazz tuba players are rare.

Range. The tuba is written in the bass clef. It has a range of F below the bass clef to B-flat, on the second line from the bottom of the bass clef. Many tuba players can play higher. See example 23.

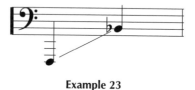

Example 23

Brass Combinations for the Studio

Budget is a consideration in choosing the right instrumental combination. With a modest budget, two trumpets, one tenor trombone, and a bass trombone will sound full if scored properly. If the assignment requires a small orchestra, try to budget one or two French horns. No other instrument can produce quite the same sound.

The tuba is usually the last to be added. Most of the time a tuba player is hired because the arrangement specifically needs that sound, for example in a Dixieland piece. A tuba cannot replace a double bass in a typical orchestra setting.

WOODWINDS

Woodwind is a deceptive term, since many of the instruments in this category, for example, flutes and saxophones, are not made of wood. Woodwinds include the various flutes clarinets, oboes, English horns, bassoons, and saxophones. As with the other instrumental sections of an orchestra, the woodwinds provide unique sounds and combinations—their own color. As a group, they blend well with many other sections.

Most commercial woodwind players play two or three different woodwind instruments. This offers the arranger a wider selection of instruments, because the colors of different sections can change as a result of player diversity.

Note: Musicians who double or triple receive additional session payments.

All traditional flutes are held in a horizontal position and are played by blowing into a metal mouthpiece. The family of flutes consists of piccolo, flute, alto flute, and bass flute.

Piccolo

The piccolo is the highest flute and is used in both orchestras and bands. The most familiar sounds of this instrument are the busy high countermelodies common to marches, along with high trills. The piccolo sounds one octave above the flute. The sound can be piercing, so it should be used sparingly. In most instances, there is one piccolo, but for certain effects, three and four can be used.

Generally, flute players also play the piccolo. The fingering of the piccolo is the same as the fingering of the flute, but the very low and very high notes are harder to play.

Register. The most common piccolo is pitched in C, but there is also a D-flat piccolo. The C piccolo is written in the treble clef, one octave below where it sounds. It sounds one octave above the C flute. The lowest written note is D above middle C, and the highest written note is D two octaves above the clef. See example 24.

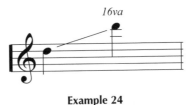

Example 24

C Flute

The most common flute is the C flute, which is a nontransposing instrument. The C flute is extensively used in jazz as well as in all forms of popular and classical music. Flute players have great dexterity on the instrument and can play almost anything. The repertoire consists of flute concertos in addition to extensive chamber music. The flute blends well with all the woodwinds and strings.

Range. The C flute is written in the treble clef and sounds where it is written. The flute sounds one octave below the piccolo. The lowest note is middle C, and the highest note is C, two octaves above the staff. See example 25.

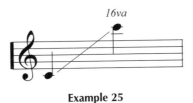

Example 25

Alto Flute

The alto flute is a warm-sounding instrument and is popular in jazz. Three or four alto flutes playing in unison produce a soothing sound. Since alto flutes are soft, the arrangement has to be sparse enough to allow for them to be heard. The alto flute takes more air to play than a C flute, so the arranger should not write parts that require as much physical dexterity as the C flute.

Range. The instrument is pitched in G and sounds a perfect fourth below where it is written. The lowest written note is middle C (which sounds a G below), and the highest written note is F above the treble clef. Some players can play higher. See example 26.

Example 26

Bass Flute

The bass flute is an unusual instrument and can add a distinctive quality to an arrangement. It takes a lot of air to generate a sound through a bass flute, so the parts written for it should not require short or fast sequences. Three or four bass flutes playing in unison make an incredible sound. As with the alto flute, since the instrument does not project well, the arrangement must be sparse if it is to be heard.

Register. The bass flute is pitched in C, written in the treble clef, and sounds one octave below where it is written. The lowest written note is middle C (sounding one octave lower), and the highest note is G above the treble clef. See example 27.

Example 27

Wooden flutes are found in most cultures. Since each culture has flutes that are unique and requires individual playing techniques, study the musical culture before writing for the instrument.

There are Irish flutes, Renaissance flutes, bamboo flutes, Native American flutes, and many other types of wooden flutes. Below are descriptions of some ethnic flutes.

Irish flute. The Irish Flute contains six holes, with the lowest note being a D above middle C; the flute will sound a D-major scale as the holes are opened, with the top note being a C-sharp. This enables the player to easily play in the keys of D major and G major, which will accommodate many traditional Irish melodies. Adding metal keys that are attached to the wood can expand the range of the flute. The flutes are made in a variety of keys.

Baroque flutes. Baroque flutes obtain an authentic sound of the period. By cross-fingering, a baroque flute player can play a full chromatic scale. Some baroque flutes have two separate joint sections, which will enable the player to tune to the baroque pitch of A-415 or the standard A-440 pitch used today.

Renaissance flutes. Renaissance flutes should be used to replicate sixteenth-century Renaissance music. The Renaissance flute is a transverse flute and was probably used from the late fifteenth century to the second half of the seventeenth century.

Boxwood was the most common material used to make Renaissance flutes, but some were made of various fruitwoods. Most tenor flutes were made in one piece, and most of the basses were made in two parts. They were made in three sizes:

- The bass flute is tuned in G minor, and the range is two octaves from G to G''
- The tenor flute is tuned in D minor; the range is two and a half octaves from D' to A'''
- Descant, or highest flute, is tuned in A' minor; sometimes the tenor plays this part.

Native American flutes. Native American flutes are made in many shapes and sizes. They can be made of cedar, redwood, or walnut. The flutes have either five or six holes and are tuned to traditional minor scales. Study the tribes and theory of Native American flute playing if trying to emulate a specific tribe.

Wooden ocarinas. Wooden ocarinas are chromatically tuned flutes made out of a variety of woods. They have an unusual oval shape.

Recorder. A recorder is held vertically and has a two-octave range. The recorder is made in many sizes. It is difficult to vary dynamics with this instrument.

Shakuhachi flutes of Japan. Shakuhachi flutes are traditionally made of bamboo (some modern ones are made of maple), are held vertically, and come in many sizes; the bamboo is taken from the very bottom of a bamboo tree. They are tuned to the key of D, which is traditional.

There are four finger holes on the front and a thumbhole on the back. The mouthpiece is open on the top of the open pipe. The player can play in a very expressive manner by using various blowing techniques and half-hole fingering.

The original Zen music for Shakuhachi is called Honkyoku and is played with bamboo flutes tuned only to the bamboo; since this is not traditional tuning and the tuning varies between instruments, Honkyoku is only played solo.

Chinese *dizi* bamboo flute (also called *d'tzu* or *ahu di*). The dizi is held like a traditional modern flute (side blown) and is made of bamboo. It has one blowhole, one membrane hole, six finger holes, and two pairs of holes in the end. Some dizis are made with seven or twelve keys, but those are not the traditional instruments. The dizi dates back to the Yuan dynasty, which was from A.D. 1279–1368.

There are two types of dizi flutes, the *bon di* and the *qun di*. In the north, the flute used in the Bon Zi Opera, located in northern China, was accompanied by the bon di. This flute is pitched higher than the qun di. The Quan Opera, located in southern China, was accompanied by the qun di.

Dizi players generally use three fingers. The average range is two octaves plus several additional notes.

Chinese xiao bamboo flute. The xiao is played vertically and provided the basic design for the Japanese Shakuhachi bamboo flute.

Peruvian pan flute (also known as *zampona*). The pan flute is made of bamboo shoots in various sizes and keys. It is one of the oldest instruments in the world. Its sound, which is beautiful and soothing yet highly dramatic, has been very popular in film music. The instrument sounds good playing either slow or fast music. The European pan flute player Zamfir is the most popular modern-day proponent of the instrument.

African flutes. Flutes are part of most African cultures. Most are made of bamboo, but other materials are used, including wood, gourds, clay, horns, and various other materials. Some are made to be played like a traditional flute (transverse), while others are held vertically. Some are round or oval. Most African flutes have two to six holes.

Didgeridoo. The didgeridoo originated in northern Australia and is recognized as "the sound of Australia." It is a long flute-like instrument made from tree trunks and limbs that are cleaned out to make the tube hollow; most are made from bamboo. It has a low sound and is often played with complex rhythm patterns. It is a popular sound in film music.

The player vibrates his lips and gently blows into the instrument while simultaneously projecting sounds of various animals with his vocal chords. Some animals are very difficult to project and replication of their sounds requires an expert.

Clarinets

All clarinets have plastic mouthpieces and a single reed attached. The instrument is held vertically. There are a variety of clarinets currently being used:

1. Clarinets are pitched in B-flat, A, and E-flat.
2. The alto clarinet is pitched in E-flat.
3. The bass clarinet is pitched in B-flat.

B-Flat Clarinet

The B-flat clarinet is the standard clarinet used in popular music. (Clarinets are built in many keys.) The clarinet has always been one of the most popular instruments in both jazz (e.g., Benny Goodman) and orchestral music. The players have facile techniques, and the instrument has a wide range. A clarinet section has a beautiful mellow sound and is perfect when a cushion to an arrangement is needed. Solo clarinet has a pure, round tone and is used extensively for solos in both classical music and jazz. In a Dixieland band, a clarinet can sound raucous, and in a ballad it can sound soothing. The clarinets blend beautifully with the other woodwinds and strings. There is an extensive repertoire written for clarinet.

Range. The B-flat clarinet is written in the treble clef and sounds one full step lower than where it is written. The lowest written note is E below the treble clef (sounding D one step below), and the highest written note is G, one octave above the treble clef. Some musicians can play higher. See example 28.

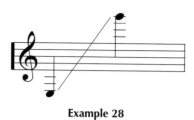

Example 28

A Clarinet

The A clarinet is written in the treble clef and has a written range of between E below middle C to G or B above the treble clef. The A clarinet sounds a minor third lower than where it is written. See example 29.

Example 29

E-Flat Clarinet

The E-flat clarinet is small and has a more piercing timbre than the B-flat clarinet. The E-flat clarinet is written in the treble clef and has the same written range as the A clarinet, but sounds a minor third higher. See example 30.

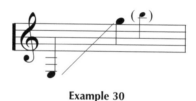

Example 30

Alto Clarinet

The alto clarinet is pitched in E-flat. The alto clarinet is written in the treble clef, with a written range from E below middle C to C through E above the treble clef. It sounds a major sixth lower than where it is written. See example 31.

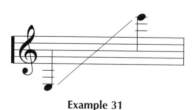

Example 31

B-Flat Bass Clarinet

The B-flat bass clarinet has a deep, resonant low end. It sounds one octave lower than the B-flat clarinet. When used in combination with other clarinets, it plays the low note—the equivalent roll the baritone saxophone plays in the saxophone section. It is also used to play low auxiliary parts in many orchestral arrangements and blends well with other low instruments, for example, celli and trombones.

   Register. The bass clarinet is written in the treble clef up a major ninth from where it sounds. The lowest written note is E below the treble clef (sounding the D below the bass clef), and the highest written note is E, on the top space of the treble clef. Some musicians can play higher. See example 32.

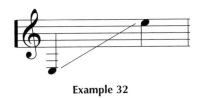

Example 32

Double Reeds

Oboe

The oboe uses a double reed, made of cane, instead of a plastic mouthpiece that holds a single reed. The oboe blends well with other woodwinds and especially sounds good playing in unison, harmony, or octaves with flutes. Oboists have great technical dexterity and can play complicated passages with ease.

Because it can make a "duck-like" sound, the instrument is also used to create a feeling of humor. The oboe is a beautiful solo instrument that can depict either sadness or playfulness. Many concertos and chamber selections have been written for the oboe.

Register. The oboe, written in the treble clef, is a nontransposing instrument and sounds where it is written. The lowest note is B-flat below middle C, and the highest note is F above the treble clef. See example 33.

Example 33

English Horn

The English horn is a tenor oboe and uses a double reed. It has a beautiful, deep, rich sound, which is best heard when playing solos.

Register. The English horn is written in the treble clef. It is pitched in F and written a perfect fifth above where it sounds. The lowest written note is B below middle C (sounding an E below the treble clef), and the highest written note is F, two octaves above the treble clef. See example 34.

Example 34

Bassoon

The bassoon is the lowest of the commonly used double reed instruments. It has a beautiful, almost muted quality. A bassoon, along with a bass clarinet, typically plays the low part in a woodwind section.

When played in its low register, it can take on the role of a comic. When playing a melody in a high register, it can sound beautiful. The bassoon blends well with almost any instrument in the orchestra.

There are a limited number of concertos and chamber pieces written for the bassoon when compared with what has been written for flutes and clarinets.

Register. The bassoon, written in the bass clef, is a nontransposing instrument that sounds where it is written. The lowest note is B-flat below the bass clef, and the highest note is E-flat on the top space of the treble clef. See example 35.

Example 35

Contrabassoon

The contrabassoon is written an octave above where it sounds and is pitched in C. The lowest written note is B-flat below the bass clef, and the highest written note is E-flat above middle C. This is an unusual instrument in a commercial orchestra setting. See example 36.

Example 36

Woodwind Combinations for the Studio

Many woodwind combinations work well. The following are some suggestions:

1. Flutes and clarinets playing in octaves
2. Clarinet, oboe, and C flute playing in unison
3. C flute and oboe in unison or playing harmony
4. Flute, oboe, clarinet, and bassoon or bass clarinet playing in harmony
5. Oboe and clarinet playing in octaves
6. Clarinet with bass clarinet or bassoon playing one octave below
7. Two flutes playing in harmony
8. Two oboes playing in harmony
9. Two bassoons and two clarinets playing in harmony
10. Flute playing the highest octave, oboe playing one octave below, and clarinet one octave below the oboe

Almost any combination will sound good. Many of these instruments blend well with other sections of the orchestra. For example:

1. Flutes with violins
2. Bassoons with celli
3. Bassoons and bass clarinet with bass trombone and tuba
4. Clarinets with almost any instrument
5. Muted trumpets and flutes

SAXOPHONES

Even though saxophones are not made of wood, they are considered woodwinds but are listed in their own category. They have plastic mouthpieces with a single reed attached.

The saxophones used in contemporary music are soprano, alto, tenor, baritone, bass, and contrabass. (The bass and contrabass saxophones are rarely used, except for specific purposes.)

Saxophones are not considered a standard orchestral instrument. In modern concert music, composers (e.g., Richard Strauss and Bizet) have used saxophones. There are many chamber works and concertos written for them. They have always been an intrinsic part of popular orchestras and jazz groups as well as concert and marching bands. French composers, to create the dominant sound in French band music, have used saxophones extensively.

The typical saxophone section consists of two altos, two tenors, and a baritone. In unusual circumstances, the baritone player doubles with a bass saxophone. The soprano saxophone has become quite a popular instrument, especially in jazz (e.g., John Coltrane).

The saxophone section has a beautiful blend. When music is written for it in tight harmony, the section can sound like one instrument; few other sections sound as cohesive. Another unique section sound results from writing octaves and unisons. Parts can be written to be played at lightning speed, because professional saxophone players have extraordinary technique. This is partially owing to the fact that the saxophone is the easiest of the woodwinds to blow into in order to create a sound. Saxophones blend with almost any section. They are especially rich sounding when played in the middle to low octaves along with the strings. The baritone is often written with the bass trombone and tuba. Most commercial saxophone players also play clarinet and flute; some also play double reeds, for example, oboe, English horn, and bassoon.

All saxophones have the same written range and are fingered in the same manner.

Soprano Saxophone

The soprano saxophone is the highest-pitched of the instruments, and it is shaped more like a clarinet than the other saxophones. It is mostly used as a solo instrument, especially in jazz. Having a beautiful mellow sound, it is also very effective in playing solo parts in film orchestras, because the sound does not interfere with the dialogue the way, for example, a trumpet would.

Register. The soprano, written in the treble clef, is pitched in the key of B-flat and sounds one full tone below where it is written. The lowest written note is B-flat below middle C (sounding A-flat below middle C), and the highest written note is F, one octave above the treble clef. See example 37.

Example 37

Alto Saxophone

The alto saxophone usually plays the lead part in a saxophone section. (Sometimes the lead is played by the soprano saxophone.) There are typically two altos in a section. The second alto normally plays the part directly below the lead alto; sometimes one of the tenors plays the second part and the second alto plays the third harmony. The alto players are usually good jazz soloists and play solos in big band arrangements.

Register. The E-flat alto saxophone is pitched in the key of E-flat. It is written in the treble clef one sixth above where it sounds. The lowest written note is B-flat below middle C (sounding a D-flat below middle C in the bass clef), and the highest written note is F one octave above the treble clef. See example 38.

Example 38

Tenor Saxophone

The B-flat tenor saxophone is pitched in the key of B-flat. It usually plays the third and fourth parts in a typical section. This is arguably the most popular jazz saxophone. Tenors sound especially good with trombones. In fact, two tenors and two trombones can sound like a trombone section.

Register. The B-flat tenor saxophone, written in the treble clef, sounds a ninth below where it is written. The lowest written note is B-flat below middle C (sounding A-flat on the first space of the bass clef), and the highest written note is F one octave above the treble clef.

Baritone Saxophone

The E-flat baritone saxophone usually plays the lowest note in the section. It is also effective at playing solos, primarily in jazz and R & B. It produces a unique rich, deep, raspy sound that cannot be duplicated by any other instrument.

> The baritone is not often used for jazz solos, but there have been some extraordinary jazz musicians who have made the instrument popular, such as Jerry Mulligan, Pepper Adams, and Ronnie Cuber.

Register. The E-flat baritone saxophone is written in the treble clef and sounds one octave and a sixth below where it is written. The lowest written note is B-flat below middle C (sounding D-flat below the bass clef), and the highest written note is F, one octave above the treble clef.

Bass Saxophone

The B-flat bass saxophone is the least used of the modern saxophones. It has an amazingly deep sound and should be reserved for special use.

Register. The B-flat bass saxophone is written in the treble clef and sounds two octaves and one full tone below where it is written. The lowest written note is B-flat below middle C (sounds A-flat below the bass clef), and the highest written note is B-flat above the treble clef. See example 39.

Example 39

Saxophone Combinations for the Studio

If there is a limited budget, an alto and two tenors or two altos and a tenor will have a good blend. Generally, a baritone will be the last saxophone to be added, unless that particular sound is generic to the style of arrangement, for example fifties rock and roll. Saxophones are pliable instruments and work with almost any orchestral or band combination.

GENERAL COMBINATIONS FOR THE STUDIO

Some budgets only allow for a small horn section. The following are some examples of sections that will blend well:

1. Two trumpets, a tenor sax, and a baritone sax
2. One trumpet, one tenor, playing in octaves or in unison
3. Two trumpets and two trombones
4. One trumpet, one alto sax and one tenor sax
5. Three trumpets, a tenor sax, and one tenor trombone

If the part is well written, various combinations will sound good.

CONCLUSION

Arranging and orchestration provide the colors for the composer. The arranger must be careful not to "over-arrange." When too much is written, the arrangement tends to sound muddled and has a lack of clarity. In the creation of a jingle, the arrangement should surround and enhance the melody and the lyric, not overpower it.

The composer should try to internalize the sound of the arrangement while composing and then write the arrangement or have the arrangement written down by a copyist. All composers should study arranging and orchestration and learn as many styles as possible. The more styles an arranger can tackle, the more assignments he or she is able to accept. Without arrangements and a choice of instrumentation to add colors, music could become boring.

ASSIGNMENTS

1. Compose music for a fifteen-second commercial (make up a product) and write three rhythm section arrangements for it, each with a different style.
2. Write a short string arrangement followed by a brass and woodwind arrangement (without strings), with a rhythm section as the foundation.

7

Jingle Writing

Note: Even though the term *jingle* is offensive to some composers, songs for commercials will be referred to here as jingles.

The recorded history of advertisement music begins only when music printing became inexpensive.

During the 19th century the street cry was transmuted into the Jingle on trade cards and in newspaper and magazine advertisements. Some companies advertised on sheet music and in music collections; others published their own music. In early 20th-century England Beecham's Pills issued a series of portfolios which included popular songs, folksongs, numbers from operettas and other light classical selections, and excerpts from Handel and Mendelssohn oratorios, all interspersed with advertising copy and music specifically intended to promote Beecham's product. Though lacking obvious jingles, the portfolios included dances such as the "Guinea a Box Polka" (alluding to the price of Beecham's Pills), the "St Helen's Waltz" (that being where they were manufactured), the "Beecham's Chimes Galop" and "Beecham's March to Health".

—www.grovemusic.com

Musical Commercial Saves Wheaties from Extinction

Wheaties made advertising history as the first product to feature a singing commercial on network radio. Its first airing took place on Christmas Eve 1926. The soon-to-be famous "Have You Tried Wheaties" jingle was sung by four male singers known as "The Wheaties Quartet." The commercial was a barometer on how popular Wheaties was with the people. Sales increased in areas where the people heard the commercial. Unfortunately, the musical commercial was heard in only a very limited area of the United States. In those regions where the musical commercial wasn't heard, sales floundered badly.

With the product's sagging popularity, General Mills, the makers of Wheaties, came within a whisker of discontinuing the production and selling of Wheaties. At a company staff meeting, an advertising executive for Wheaties offered the suggestion that would save the cereal. He stated that since the sales were good in those regions where the Wheaties musical commercial was heard, why not air the commercial in as many regions of the country as possible. In a nutshell, the musical commercials were aired, sales improved, and Wheaties would quickly become one of the most popular breakfast cereals.

Note: In 1841 the first advertising agency opened in the United States. The name of the company was Volney B. Palmer, and they were located in Philadelphia.

—www.old-time.com/commercials/wheaties.html

Jingles are miniature songs. In the 1940s Pepsi-Cola broadcast the first national jingle, "Pepsi-Cola Hits the Spot." Some jingles have become popular songs, for example, "I'd Like to Teach the World to Sing" was originally a jingle for Coke. Many popular songs have been used as jingles, for example, "Like a Rock" for Chevrolet.

Most popular songs have a buildup to a chorus (or hook), which is memorable. Since the average song is three minutes long, the composer has time to build the compositional structure. Jingle writing does not afford the composer that same luxury; a jingle must grab the attention of the audience immediately. Most jingles are catchy and easy to remember, or they are not successful.

Soft drink companies have had a long tradition of using jingles as the center of their advertising, for example, Coke and Pepsi, as have electronic companies like General Electric (GE, We Bring Good Things to Life).

The elements that make a song catchy are:

1. More conjunct (stepwise) motion than disjunctive (skips) motion in the melodic structure.
2. Easy to remember after the first hearing.
3. Easy for the average person to sing along with.

Jingle lyrics can create an image for a company. The advertising agency spends a painstaking amount of time developing the most effective lyric for a jingle. The message must be clear and immediate. It is not unusual for an agency to spend months refining lyrics and creating alternative lyrics for alternative campaigns.

Since most advertising campaigns mirror contemporary society, many creatives use examples of popular songs to demonstrate the style of jingle they would like for their commercial. The agency and client are concerned about appealing to the demographic and/or psychographic psyche of their customer and/or potential customer. They are therefore discriminating about the style of music they choose. Not being offensive to their target audience is of great concern. Focus group testing becomes an important factor in helping to choose the final commercial and the final music. The focus group is asked to comment on the various components of a potential commercial; if an element, for example, music, is not well received, the agency will most likely change that part of the commercial.

The Ford Motor Company conducted research to see what kind of music, if any, their pickup truck customers listened to. They found that their customers generally preferred country music over other genres. This kind of information and other similar information that helps develop a profile of their consumer is essential to advertising agencies when developing a campaign strategy.

For most popular national products, several music houses are hired to submit jingles. After extensive focus group testing, the final music is picked. The commercial or commercials are then tested in a region and, if successful, are aired regionally and nationally. (This is the typical procedure when working on a national jingle campaign.)

LICENSING POPULAR SONGS

There has also been a long tradition of licensing popular songs for commercials because of their familiarity to the consumer. This helps the audience to immediately associate the product with the song. Sometimes, agency copywriters write their own lyrics to a popular melody; other clients use the song in its original form but edit the format so an announcer can read the client's message over a musical bed. Some agencies license the original recordings and fade them at the end of the commercial without any editing.

High-profile artists such as Michael Jackson, Sting, Britney Spears, and Elton John have written and/or performed on commercials. When music celebrities were first used on commercials, many musicians believed they were selling out—losing their credibility. As time passed, the exposure was so rewarding that the stigma was lifted. Album sales have soared after artists have appeared in well-produced, high-profile commercials.

Celebrities know exactly what the commercial is going to look like and sound like before they agree to participate in it. All managers and agents are concerned with protecting their client's image and therefore build in safeguards to the agency contracts. An artist will walk off the set if he feels his credibility is in jeopardy.

These artists receive very large fees for their participation, which is definitely a motivating factor. Compensation can be in the millions of dollars, for stars like Britney Spears and Michael Jackson.

In 2002, a group from Europe called Dirty Vegas scored a big success with the song "Days Go By," which was used on a campaign for the Mitsubishi Eclipse automobile. The agency spent $30 million in media buying, therefore providing great exposure for the song. The song jetted to the top of the dance charts in Billboard Magazine and broke through to mainstream radio.

This shows the power of advertising; the song would never have received this attention on the radio because it did not fit into the general format of pop radio in the United States. When listeners request to hear a song, as in this case, radio has to play it to satisfy its listeners.

Listeners call radio stations to request songs, which is why most radio stations do not announce what is being played. Stations want listeners to call so they can determine which songs are popular with their listening audience.

The first question that is asked at a record label after a song is first played on the radio is, "How were the phones?" This is the industry expression for "How many calls were received at the station immediately after the record was played?" Sometimes, if the phone calls are meager, the programmer will not continue to play the record; when the inquiries are numerous, she will sometimes add the song to the regular play list, which means it gets a progressive increase in airplay, depending on its increase in popularity, which is measured by sales. If sales do not result from continuous airplay yet the "phones" keep coming into the request line at the radio station, this is what is known in the industry as *a turntable hit*.

This, obviously, does not benefit the record label but helps the commercial because of song recognition and continued identification of the product.

Between obtaining a synchronization license from a music publisher and obtaining the rights to use an original recording, the client could pay in the millions for a very popular song.

There are many forms of rights agreements. For example, a song might only be limited to a category, for example, soft drinks. The same song could simultaneously be used in a car commercial because it is a noncompetitive product category. The licensing fee to exclusively license a song is substantially higher.

The rights might call for a one-year term with a specified number of uses during that term; there could be built-in options with an additional fee schedule.

Rights agreements can become complicated and therefore should be negotiated by an expert. Most large agencies have in-house attorneys who negotiate the deals with music publishers and record companies. There are private clearance agencies that will clear and research song licenses.

Agreements are not standard and are therefore always negotiated.

JINGLES

Many successful songwriters do not write well-crafted jingles. Writing miniature songs is a special craft that requires the ability to compress the song form.

A good jingle writer can write a thirty-second hook, meaning both the verse and the chorus are both easy to remember.

The average television jingle runs thirty seconds; most of those commercials have fifteen-second versions. Some fifteen-second versions are called "lifts," meaning that they are edited from a longer version. The average radio commercial is sixty seconds, which means that the jingle has to work in a fifteen-second format. Just as with an underscore, a composer might write a jingle that works well in thirty seconds but not when it's edited to fifteen seconds. The composer must be aware of this potential dilemma during the writing process. The agency will expect the jingle to be adaptable.

Most campaigns require the music not only to fit in different timings but also to work in various arranging styles. Most national high-profile advertising campaigns will run at least a year, and the agency will most likely film a variety of commercials based around a central idea called a "pool out."

This suggests a need for musical variety. The jingle will most likely go through many incarnations before airing. The agencies will sometimes request hearing three or four styles of arrangements before choosing the final song. The client will most likely be spending millions of dollars in airtime and will not take a chance that the jingle is not adaptable.

Most successful jingles have a very strong "hook" line that becomes a musical logo for the product. (The lyric of the logo is generally used in the accompanying print campaign.) Sometimes, the melody of the jingle is played instrumentally (called the bed), and only the hook line is sung as a tag line or intermittently throughout the commercial, with copy being read in between the singing.

For example: The announcer says, "The _____ is the safest car on the road," and the singers sing, "Buckle up for Safety." Then the announcer says, "The car has been voted the safest car on the road for the past three years," followed by the singers singing, "Buckle up for Safety." This format then continues throughout the commercial.

LYRICS WRITTEN BY THE COPYWRITERS

The agency copywriters generally write the lyrics for jingles. Frequently, this creates a problem for the composer, because most agency writers are not lyricists. The writer is usually given a "laundry list" of topics to be included in the lyric. Many copywriters literally just write a "list" with a minimum of lyrical cohesiveness. They try to incorporate too many thoughts in a short period of time, not realizing that the lyric must fit a tempo and predetermined length.

The best approach for the composer is to point out the lyrical problems before writing the melody. Writers will generally make adjustments after hearing a logical musical explanation of why the lyric needs to be edited. The problems occur when the client insists that all of its copy points are covered in one lyric. Sometimes, in order to fit the time restrictions, the tempo becomes so fast that it is impossible for the audience to understand the words. Plea with the creatives to make further lyrical adjustments; sometimes adjectives or nouns can be removed without affecting the meaning of the lyric.

> During recording, every word must be understood or a rerecord is inevitable, at the expense of the music company. The number one objective during the recording session is to obtain lyrical clarity. Hire singers who are used to singing jingles, because they realize the importance of good diction.

LYRICS WRITTEN BY THE MUSIC HOUSE LYRICISTS

If the music company is asked to write the lyrics, it is usually by a small agency in a local market. It is rare for a large agency to request lyrics from a music house.

If the assignment includes writing lyrics, hire a lyricist with advertising experience. There are freelance writers with lyrical experience in commercials; they understand advertising music and generally know how to analyze an assignment. Stay in close contact with the agency creatives while the lyrics are being written. The lyrics are the key to success. If the client does not buy the lyrics, the agency will hire another music house. The lyrics are always approved by the agency prior to recording a demo.

Because the main ingredient in a lyric or advertising campaign is a hook line, the lyricist must become familiar with the advertising strategy of the product and write a line that will satisfy the agency and client. Since the lyric is such a crucial part of the strategy, it is best when the agency writer feeds the line to the music house and then the lyricist writes the lyric using that line. Most agency writers are happy to let the music company lyricist edit the lyric and make it as musical as possible. It is rare that egos get in the way of good advertising.

DEMOS

The process of developing jingles and submitting them to the client and agency is the same as submitting underscore demos. As a general rule, try to submit three pieces of music:

1. Write what the creatives ask for.
2. Write what you want to write (assuming you have a different conception than the creatives).
3. Write additional music that is in a different musical direction.

Agencies traditionally offer a low budget for demos. Because of the advanced technology, as with underscores, demos are no longer really demos in the traditional sense; most demos sound like finals. If a jingle is chosen to go on the air, the changes that are made to the demo are generally to adapt the jingle to fit the film and maybe add some performers.

APPROACHING A JINGLE

Writing a jingle is not unlike writing an underscore. The creatives will generally give the jingle writer a storyboard. The storyboard contains a scene-by-scene pictorial description of the commercial with the lyrics written under each cell. The storyboard is laid out exactly like a storyboard used for underscoring; it contains camera directions, detailed drawings of each frame of picture, lyrics, and dialogue.

The following is a list of ideas that might help the composer when writing a jingle:

Clarity. As previously mentioned, the main objective is lyrical clarity. This also applies to the production of the recording and the performances. An acceptable recording is difficult to achieve if the composition is not well written. The composer should be aware that certain words "sing better" when the proper number of syllables and the appropriate rhythmic values are assigned to each word. For example, if the word has more than one syllable, assign a note to each syllable. If the word is *concentrate*, it is better to have three eighth notes than three sixteenth notes or only two notes; when sung, the word will be easier to understand.

Notate rhythmic values. Assign rhythmic values to each word before writing the actual pitches. This will aid in making the lyric sound conversational. It will also help in emphasizing the proper words. The composer should mark Xs on the score paper with rhythmic values (eighth notes, sixteenth notes, etc.) and indicate whether the note should go up or down. Write the lyric under each rhythmic value and then write the melody under each rhythmic value.

The product name is the most important word. The main concern of the client is to sell their product. The note or notes assigned to the product name must stand out so that the audience remembers the product.

Most jingles have a logo phrase that is repeated several times throughout the jingle, called a hook. If the audience cannot remember the hook, the jingle will fail. The composer must be certain that the musical highlight of the jingle is the product name. If the lyric writer does not repeat the name of the product often enough to help create an image, suggest that the name be added more often. Sometimes the best solution is for the composer to make corrections and then play them for the creatives and get the changes approved. Several problems can occur:

1. The commercial may be too long if some of the original lyric is not deleted.
2. It may not be acceptable to delete certain sections of the lyric. The client might insist that certain ideas remain in the lyric. Experimentation can aid in reaching an acceptable solution.

Melodic simplicity. Melodic simplicity is what makes a song catchy. The client will expect to hear a melody that is easy to remember. Since commercials are short, try to make the entire jingle a hook—easy to remember. it is hoped that the audience will remember the song from the first to last note. (Sometimes this is not possible because of the manner in which the lyric is written.)

The song should not be too rangy. Keep the notes within singing range of the average person, so they can sing along. Most of the time, the use of conjunctive motion makes a melody easier to remember.

There are exceptions to this general rule. An agency might ask for a jazz jingle or operatic song-form, which means that they are just looking for a well-written piece of music. When an agency is expecting to hear a catchy song, they will usually tell the composer. If the assignment is to write a traditional jingle, make it catchy, otherwise, just *make it good.*

Donuts. Most jingles have "donuts" (music only) primarily in the middle of the jingle. This space, or donut, is typically used for the actors or announcer to deliver a message. During the donut, play the vocal melody instrumentally so that the audience is still hearing the main theme during the dialogue. The strategy is to aid the audience in remembering the melody, which in turn helps them to remember the product name.

Harmony. Most jingles are harmonically simple. This does not mean that the song has to sound trite or redundant. Many of the most popular songs have simple chord structures. If the melody is interesting and catchy, the song will be successful.

Arrangement and orchestration. Since the style of music will be predetermined, keep the arrangement and orchestration authentic. Hire an arranger who is familiar with the style. If it is supposed to sound like rock and roll, use a rock and roll rhythm section and not a full orchestra playing out-of-character parts. The arrangement should be interesting and creative. Since most advertising jingles mirror currently popular songs, listen to and analyze the structure and arrangements of the songs closest to what the client is looking for.

> Many jingle writers are not arrangers. They generally specialize in composing in this highly competitive and lucrative musical genre.

Check the key with the singer(s) before writing the arrangement. The wrong key can create serious problems at a recording session. If the key is out of range or sounds strained, the song will fail.

This key also affects the harmonic structure of the arrangement. For example, if the key is changed after the arrangement has been completed, the woodwind or string orchestration might require inversions because the harmonies might be too high or too low in their original inversions.

To avoid this problem, before writing the arrangement, make certain that the agency has approved the choice for the lead singer; then audition the lead singer (on the telephone) and choose the most comfortable key. If the track requires some improvisation, do not make the key too high because the singer will have no place to go.

> All singers have a break in their voices. It usually occurs between their chest or middle vocal range and their head voice, their high range. If the key is not correct, the melody could lie where the voice breaks. This problem must be avoided.
>   Most singers with technical training will not have a noticeable break. Ask the singers if the key affects this potential problem.

If there is a solo singer, submit several demo tapes to the agency so they can choose the voice that attracts them. Most creatives are particular about the choice of singer(s). Remember, this is personal taste. Three great singers could be submitted for the job, but only one might appeal to the creatives and to the client.

> In rare instances an agency will request that more than one lead singer record on the final music track. This usually happens for several reasons:
>
> 1. The creatives want to choose the finalist after hearing several complete vocals.
> 2. They might want to run the commercial with two or more lead singers to create variety.
> 3. The creatives might want a female lead and a male lead. (In this case, the arrangement will probably have to be copied in two different keys. Be aware of the potential inversion problems previously discussed.)
> 4. The creatives might want to experiment with a duet—two females, two males, or one of each.

Male or female lead singer. Find out if the lead singer should be male, female, or possibly a duet with alternating lines or duets. There are many ways to write vocal arrangements. Sometimes the lyric will dictate the form.

If the objective is to make the singer(s) sound full, double the vocal(s); if the objective is intimacy, do not double the vocal(s) and have the singer stand close to the microphone. Most experienced studio singers have good microphone technique and a sense of how to achieve the objective of the music producer. They will generally make suggestions on how to achieve the musical goal.

Background singers. The decision to hire background singers is both creative and financial. Most jingles need backgrounds to fill out the parts and create excitement. Jingles are generally structured with the verse being sung by a solo voice and the background singers entering during the chorus, which generally emphasizes the name of the product. When hiring background singers there are several crucial factors to consider:

1. They must all have perfect intonation.
2. Their voices must be similar in character so they blend well.
3. They all must have a feel for the style of music being recorded.
4. Good phrasing is of utmost importance.

5. If there is a large group of singers, always double the melody before doubling anything else. This will keep the group sounding balanced.
6. Make sure that they all sing at relatively the same volume. If they don't, they will not sound balanced on the recording.
7. If arranging for a large chorus, try to have the same number of singers on each part. This will make the chorus sound balanced. Putting more singers on the lead part will make the melody louder, which is sometimes desirable.

The number of singers has to be cleared by the agency and client before the recording session. The cost in both fees and residual payments is calculated based on the media buy. If the music track is a jingle, this is not normally a problem. If the singers are primarily used as a part of the band and not featured, there might be a problem. Some large clients have policies concerning the use of singers. One of the largest advertisers does not allow any voices to be used on an underscoring. They feel that the cost of residuals makes it prohibitive.

> The author once used three singers in an underscoring. The producer failed to inform the author that it was the policy of the advertiser not to use singers on an underscoring. After the track was completed, the author had to remix the track and eliminate the singers. Those missing parts were transcribed for synthesizers.

Overdubbing. Most backgrounds are doubled or tripled during the recording session. Sometimes lead singers double parts. Doubling creates a full sound, which is more affective in certain musical styles.

Doubling becomes a creative choice that has to be made by the composer, arranger, and/or music producer. There are additional fees for this service. The agency must approve it, in writing, prior to the session.

> Some of these problems do not exist in states that do not require musicians and singers to belong to unions. They are more often than not paid one fee called a buyout. The agency then has the use of the jingle in perpetuity.

Hiring musicians. The choice of musicians is extremely important to the success of a commercial. As previously mentioned, authenticity is the key to success. Always try to capture the style of the jingle. For instance, if a jazz guitar player is hired to play on a rock and roll jingle, the chances are that it will not sound like a rock and roll guitar—because it isn't! It may be advantageous to hire a contractor to book the best-qualified musicians—especially if the style of music or the instrumentation is unusual.

The following are the most common compositional mistakes and should be avoided when writing jingles. Refer also to chapter 5, Underscoring (Compositional Techniques).

When writing for television, always begin the music approximately seven frames into the film and finish the music half a second before the film ends. (There are thirty video frames per second in the U.S.) The reason for this is that it takes time for the video to "roll in" and get up to speed; at the end, time is needed to get out of the film smoothly. If the music continued to the very end, the transition to the next event would be too abrupt.

Do not compose a jingle that is too long to fit in a shorter version of the same commercial. The most common assignment is to write a thirty-second jingle that can be shortened to fifteen seconds. Depending on the musical needs of the film, one suggestion is to write short thematic fragments, which are easily adaptable and lend themselves to modulation, which helps to keep the composition interesting. Another suggestion is to write a theme that is no longer than twelve seconds. This leaves room for an introduction and ending in the fifteen-second version and room for expansion in the longer version. (This is based on the assumption that the tempos of the various versions are the same.)

Before writing, experiment with a variety of tempos; each commercial included in a campaign might require a different arrangement and different tempo. This will help determine the flexibility of the theme. Not all jingles adapt well.

Sometimes it is difficult to write an extended jingle that will work in its original form in all required variations. In this case, make sure that the first or second part of the jingle can be used as an independent theme. This is a common problem when compressing the music to fit in a ten-second version. The theme might work well in thirty- and fifteen-second versions, but there is not enough time to fit the entire piece in nine seconds. A solution might be to lift an individual section of the original theme. The audience will still identify with the original full theme, because they will recognize the phrase that has been used.

Most agencies accept this practice because they realize that the original composition would have to be compromised to solve the problem. Since most of the airplay will probably be the thirty- and fifteen-second versions, they are willing to make this compromise.

> Film composer Danny Elfman always tries to write short, identifiable themes so that a four- or five-note excerpt heard within a cue will immediately create an identity for the audience, for example, those written for *Batman* or *Star Wars*.

Some jingles, even though well constructed, do not adapt well to different styles and tempos. Even though it might fit other styles and tempos, the composition might only sound good in its original form. If the theme is going to have to be adapted, experiment before presenting it to the agency.

Once the jingle has been approved, the integrity of the composition must remain. A problem can result if the composition is not adaptable to different arrangements. The agency and client will certainly notice that the theme is missing or incomplete. If the theme has to be compressed for other versions, let the creatives know before writing.

After approving the theme and discussing the various versions, the agency might add another version. If the theme will not fit in its entirety, present the best solution possible and explain the problem to the creatives. Most of the time there is an acceptable solution.

The composition might contain odd time signatures, which could make the rhythm or melody feel unnatural. This normally occurs if the composer wants to start a new musical statement over a particular part of the film. For example, if a scene changes from pictures of mountains to the inside of a department store, the composer will most likely want the singers to start a new section over the scene change rather than continue the previous line. The bar prior to the scene change might require an odd time signature so the overall timing is correct. (Ideas for solving these problems are discussed in chapter 5.)

When scoring to the film, listen closely to the frequency range of the dialogue. A common error is to write in the same frequency range as the actors or announcer. In the case of jingles, this applies to all instrumental sections. When this happens, the composition will often sound busy and cluttered. One solution is to choose octaves that will not conflict with the voices. Think of the dialogue as being a part of the orchestration. This also has to be taken into account when writing a theme that runs throughout a commercial. Sometimes, sparse writing can be an effective solution—*there are no rules.* Whatever works best is what should be used.

PRODUCTION TIPS

Always separate all of the elements of the recorded track. In addition to a full mix, mix each of the following elements separately:

1. Instrumental only track
2. Lead vocal only track
3. Background only track

It is sometimes advisable to separate the tracks even more. Try to anticipate potential mix problems and act accordingly.

More often than not, the agency will request a remix. Having these elements separated enables the music company to work quickly and not lose the sound of the original mix. For example, if the agency wants the lead singer to resing the lead, just overdub the lead singer over the premixed background track.

The most common reasons for a remix are:

Lyrical clarity. If the lyrics are not easily understood, a resing will always be required. Diction is always of paramount concern when recording vocals for a commercial.

Creative reasons. The lyrics have to be changed for creative reasons. The client will generally request copy and possibly lyric changes up until the airdate.

Legal changes. The lyrics might have to be changed for legal reasons. Agency attorneys always check the legality of lyrics and copy. There are many subtle problems that will only be caught by experts. Specific rules have been devised by the U.S. government to protect the public and are known as truth in advertising.

POINTERS

Hire a recording engineer who specializes in recording commercials. She is used to working quickly and will save the music company money in both her hourly fee and studio time.

Mixing commercials is a specialty, and record engineers do not necessarily know how to mix commercials. Recording engineers have the luxury of time—not so with commercials. There is almost always time pressure to finish a commercial because it will be shipped to the stations. Music is generally the last creative element to be added to the commercial before the final film or radio mix.

Vocals have to be absolutely clear and equalized specifically for broadcasting. The tracks should be compressed so that they are present at low listening levels. Always mix on small speakers and at a low listening level. The objective is to try to replicate the sound of an average home television and radio; if time permits, always bring home a copy and test it on a car sound system and an average home system. The mix must sound good under any conditions—if not, *remix*.

Hire professional, flexible, and cooperative singers. Because clarity and expression are so important, it is common for the agency creatives to record many takes, which include minor changes; for example, a creative might say, "I can't hear the T on the word *it*." Jingle singers are used to this and are generally good tempered and know how to deal with agency people.

When hiring background singers, it is important that their voices blend well. Lead singers are not necessarily good background singers and vice versa. If needed, ask the singers for recommendations.

Hire musicians who are experienced in recording jingles. They are generally accustomed to the pressure and are very fast in the studio. Some studio players, who only play on records, are not as quick. The longer the musicians are in the studio, the more the session costs. The overage is generally deducted from the music company's budget.

Find out the technical format required by the agency to be used for the final layback of music onto the film/tape. DAT used to be the preferred format, but since CD and DVD burning has become standard, they now seem to be the preferred formats. Some editors will ask for an audio file, for example, AIFF or WAVE.

The following is my interview with Dr. Patricia Fleitas, Director of Choral Studies at Florida Atlantic University in Boca Raton, Florida:

Question: "How does a nonsinger learn to coach a singer?"

Patricia: "From a stylistic standpoint and a musical standpoint [it is advantageous] if the singer has technical knowledge. If the person knows what they are doing with their voice, then the musician who is a nonsinger can still coach in the musical aspect of the production. For example, a jazz specialist doesn't have to be a vocalist to teach and coach a jazz-style production, the same way that in Classical music the vocal coach, most of the time, is a nonsinger."

Question: "How do you deal with singers who are not technically trained?"

Patricia: "There is a lot of natural talent. [The singer should be] accurate for the style, sing in tune, and the production of the voice [should be] nonoffensive. A lot of the times when singers have intonation problems, the issue is technical. You have to understand the instrument to negotiate the music . . . to accommodate the score."

Question: "How do you help a singer improve their intonation?"

Patricia: "The first thing to look for is what they are doing physically. Look at breath support . . . on how they are inhaling the breath and how they are supporting the voice. The next thing is how the mechanics [of voice] are working. A depressed larynx can be one reason for intonation problems, misplacement of a vowel, an overmodification of a vowel sound, a lack of articulation. Breath is at the center of all of this."

Question: "Can you help a singer who cannot hear that their intonation is not accurate?"

Patricia: "That is a problem with musicianship. I think we are limited in how much we can help. If [the singer] is young, we can expose them to listening and that will help. I heard that you can increase the musical IQ of a child up until grade four, and the best way to do so is through a cappella singing."

Question: "Is there a way to teach singers to blend?"

Patricia: "Absolutely. The way to blend sounds is to line up the vowel placements, the vowel shapes, and the articulation of the consonants. In any kind of ensemble the performers have to listen to each other. I think of the voice in terms of colors, and I feel that the amount of colors in each individual voice is a very big palette . . . by the time we put each individual's pallet of colors in an ensemble, we have a canvas of colorful sound that is infinite."

Question: "How do you work around the break point in a singer's voice—going from a chest voice to a head voice?"

Patricia: "That is done in the training studio, not in the coaching. You even out the registration, meaning, you even out the voice from the top down without any breaks. I classify a voice not necessarily by the range but by where the voice sounds the prettiest."

Question: "Do you feel that all popular singers should have technical training?"

Patricia: "I do, because what I think technical training provides is health . . . too many singers go for style [before they have technique]."

Question: "Many popular singers feel it would be a detriment to study voice because it would change or maybe ruin their style. Do you agree with that?"

Patricia: "No, but I can understand why they feel that way. When you hear someone like Pavarotti or Placido Domingo singing something in the popular genre, it sounds very operatic." (She added that style does not have to change by learning to sing correctly and learning not to damage the voice.)

VOCAL RANGES

The five main categories for singers are soprano, alto, tenor, baritone, and bass. Most commercial female singers have ranges between soprano and alto, and most male singers have ranges between the tenor and baritone ranges.

> If the tessitura (predominate pitch range) of the piece is high, check with the singer to make sure he or she can sing it comfortably. Most singers have a difficult time singing in the top of their range for long periods of time; the best vocal range is where the vocalist is most comfortable.

The following are average ranges. Some singers can sing lower or higher than the compasses outlined below.

Soprano. The average soprano (female) has a range from middle C to A above the treble clef. Some singers can sing up to a high C. The parts are written in the treble clef and sound where they are written. See example 40.

Example 40

Alto. The average alto (female) has a range from G below middle C to C or D above middle C. Some altos can sing as high as an F. The parts are written in the treble clef and sound where they are written. See example 41.

Example 41

Tenor. The average tenor (male) has a range from C below middle C to A above middle C. Some high tenors can sing a C one octave above middle C. The parts are written in the treble clef and sound one octave lower than they are written. See example 42.

Example 42

Baritone. The average baritone (sometimes called a bass baritone) has a range from F one octave below middle C to F above middle C. Parts are written in the bass clef and sound where they are written. See example 43.

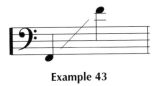

Example 43

Bass. The average bass (male) has a range from E or D, one octave below middle C, to E-flat above middle C. The parts are written in the bass clef and sound where they are written. See example 44.

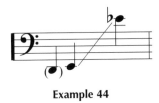

Example 44

CONCLUSION

Jingles are the most lucrative musical form in commercials. The fees are higher than for underscores and so are the residual payments. This makes jingle writing a highly competitive and profitable field. Successful jingle writers usually devote their careers to only writing jingles. It is an unusual skill and takes a long time to master.

Here is my interview with Marshall Grantham, creative director and composer for Russo/Grantham Productions, a commercial music house in New York City:

Question: "What is the difference between composing for radio and composing for television?"

Marshall : "Jingles for television and radio are similar because the song is the same.

"Radio is much more about creating the right mood to sit under the voice. I find radio easier because you can be more musical; there are less hit points to worry about. It's more a matter of hitting the target of the mood that they're shooting for."

Question: "How often are you asked to write the lyric for a jingle?"

Marshall : "Twenty percent of the time we are asked to write the lyrics and 30 percent of the time we are asked to smooth out the lyrics. A good copywriter overwrites and asks you to edit it and run it by me."

(Marshall said it is a good idea to ask the copywriters which "lyrics are in stone." This means to ask what has to be included in the lyric; do they want the product mentioned in the lyric? Ask specific questions.)

Question: "Do you have a procedure for writing a jingle?"

Marshall : "I'm a writer in my head. I already have the melody, the chorus, the verse before I even sit down at the keyboard."

Question: "When writing an underscore, where are potential problems with picture changes occurring on odd beats?"

Marshall : "I try not to give too many strange measures." (He tries to keep the meter the same and work around the hits that occur on odd beats. For example, he will sometimes have each new melodic section begin on the second beat rather than change the meter so that it occurs on the first beat.)

Question: "Before you record a demo, do you play the composition for the creative people?"

Marshall : "No. We go along the lines that they are not going to picture the stuff very well. We'd rather explore three or four ideas and produce them. More often than not, when we play them something in its infancy, they can't picture it."

Question: "What percentages of your recording sessions have live musicians?"

Marshall: "Not many—maybe 10 percent. Almost everything is programmed—we will still use live brass almost all the time—for finals, we try to bring in six or eight string players." (He said they combine the live strings with the synthesized strings to give it a more realistic sound.)

Question: "How many acoustic orchestras do you record in a year?"

Marshall : "None. I just did a spot where we had fourteen live players—several years ago we had forty—it hardly happens anymore."

(Referring to budgets, Marshall said they usually tell the agency if they want X number of live musicians or singers, the budget will be X, and if they want live players mixed with synthesizers the budget will be Y.)

Question: "What is your advice to young jingle writers?"

Marshall : "You are going to need good production values and a good setup (referring to a synthesizer setup). I don't think it's a world anymore where you are going to give a rough idea of jingle—there are no demos anymore (meaning the demos have to sound like final productions). You are going to need to be a good engineer, producer, and songwriter yourself—you might need to work without pay, at first—you are going to need every bit of the demo money, if you are paid, and you will want to pump it all into the demos."

Question: "What percentage of the time are you paying out more for a demo than the demo budget given by the agency?"

Marshall: "We technically lose money on every one (demos) just because we use our facilities (meaning studios)—I would say we lose money on every demo. We go for the win to make up for the loss." (Meaning there is almost always a competition to get the final job.)

Referring to underscoring:

Marshall : "Underscoring is having a knowledge of flow of picture, editing, and how to marry that sound to that picture." (He suggests that young composers tape commercials from television and score them for practice. Some composers offer to score demos for nothing just to show music companies what they can do.) "You never know, they might get lucky.

"I think that anyone getting into commercial music who can't produce and program is definitely not going to make it. It's a programming world at this point . . . maybe one in a hundred [composers who apply to his company] can compose, program, engineer, and produce.

"I think the most important thing is to be well-rounded in things you are going to need to make a living. Study the crafts of composing and arranging. I find a lot of composers are weak in arranging."

And here is my interview with two-time Grammy Award-winning lead singer Cissy Houston (leader of the Sweet Inspirations, one of the most successful background singing groups in recorded history, who sang backgrounds on more than five hundred hit records):

Question: "What is the difference between singing on a commercial and singing on a record?"

Cissy: "With commercials you have to be quick because time is money . . . they want people who are quick and give them the kind of expression that they need."

Question: "Does the fact that the lyric has to be exceptionally clear when singing a commercial affect your singing style?"

Cissy: "I don't know that it affects your singing style, because I'm fussy about my diction anyway. It just makes you kind of nervous sometimes when you have to do that kind of thing in thirty seconds or sixty seconds—you've got to get that message across the way they want you to do it. Sometimes they go over something over and over again, and sometimes they come right back to the first one, which is the best one."

Question: "On average, how many takes do you record when singing on a commercial?"

Cissy: "Maybe eight to ten." (Cissy said that sometimes the producer combines the best lines from each take to compile the final vocal.)

Question: "Since you have been so successful as a background singer, what is it you look for when hiring background singers to sing with you?"

Cissy: "I look for somebody who is quick and who is paying attention and who is on time . . . you have to have a good blend . . . people who are serious about their work . . . some people come in and want to play games—that really annoys me."

Question: "Some lead singers are not good background singers and vice versa. Since you have worn both hats, can you tell me the differences?"

Cissy: "It's really hard to be a great background singer. When it comes to backgrounds, you have to blend with other people and listen to other people singing—most people don't—they listen to themselves or just don't have that blend."

Question: "How does a young singer break into studio work?"

Cissy: "I would suggest that they learn to read [music] . . . you still have to have a good sound and soul in your voice." (She said that reading helps a singer to record faster. Since commercials always have specific budgets, all professional musicians and singers have to work quickly or they will not be hired.)

Question: "How important is it to be versatile both as a lead singer and as a background singer when doing commercials?"

Cissy: "I guess that is why I was so successful, because I think it is very important to be versatile. You have to be able to give different sounds . . . you might need to do a white sound or an operatic sound or whatever it takes—you might need to do a blues—you know what I mean?"

Question: "When you are hiring background singers, do you generally give each singer their part, or do you just sing the lead and have them come up with their own parts?"

Cissy: "I always come up with the backgrounds, unless they have certain backgrounds that they want. With the Sweet Inspirations, we would just break into harmony—we really knew what we were doing." (She said that singers with that ability are hard to find.)

Question: "How does a singer trying to break in get a demo reel together?"

Cissy: "Sing songs and show people what type of voice they have . . . do a versatile tape where they can do different things. I would suggest that would be the only way that I see that you can do it. Commercials are very hard to break into and it's a tight-knit situation . . . they're very, very guarded."

Question: "Do you think that most young singers should have a vocal coach so they learn to sing properly?"

Cissy: "I really do . . . [some] they scream and that's not singing . . . I work on feelings, and that's what I like to give."

Question: "Is there any advice you would like to offer young singers?"

Cissy: "Just go to school and learn—that's the easy way—but don't lose your feeling."

ASSIGNMENTS

1. Write a thirty-second lyric for a make-believe product. Make sure that there is a "hook" line—a strong chorus. Make sure the key is correct for the lead singer and vocal group.
2. Write a melody with chords and show how the jingle could be adapted to two other styles and tempos. Write several condensed arrangements.

Composing for Radio Commercials

RADIO COMMERCIALS VS. TELEVISION COMMERCIALS

Radio commercials that require underscoring generally have wall-to-wall copy. This generally means that there is constant music. The music sometimes assumes a more "visual" element since there are no pictures. The music has to fill in the gaps because there are no visual images.

Some **television commercials** have pictures without any dialogue or voice-over. When music is featured and is considered background music, the commercial may be filled with dialogue, but the addition of pictures requires "hits" that the same radio spot might not require. Television and radio commercials can have essentially the same concept but require different music. Do not assume that the same music will work for both.

Composing for radio commercials is similar to composing for television commercials except that in some ways it is more difficult! This is due to the fact that there are no pictures. Watching a film helps the composer to create musical images of the film. Listening to actors or announcers requires the composer to use his imagination and create their own images. The composer is afforded more freedom in radio because the musical hits will not generally have to be as precise as they do in television. In some instances this opens the opportunity to compose a more cohesive piece of music because of the lack of restrictions.

If the final dialogue has not been prerecorded, ask the copywriter to record a pilot track; it will make the composing process easier. At times, it is difficult to understand the intention of the writer by only reading the script; hearing the dialogue clarifies the true meaning of the copy.

> The writer must be reminded to be accurate with the timing of her reading. It is common for writers to run long, which creates problems for the composer. Listening to the dialogue while composing is the most helpful tool.

If the agency does not provide a pilot track, ask the writer questions. Make certain that the intentions of the writer are absolutely clear. Several people reading the same script may interpret it in different ways.

The agency will sometimes want the radio music completed before recording the dialogue. The producer may want to play the music for the actors or announcer while they are recording the dialogue. The music can help establish the proper mood.

Frequently, a radio commercial contains the same basic music as the television version. The difference is usually in the length—the average radio commercial is sixty seconds, so if it is to be used for radio, the composition must be expanded from the television version.

In some instances, the television music does not work for the radio version, because the pictures enhance the effectiveness of the music. Writing new music can be difficult because the composer has to reconceptualize a commercial that has basically the same meaning as the television version. The best advice is *not* to listen to the television music and instead compose as if it were a new spot.

APPROACH

If the commercials are recorded only for radio, the composer must initiate the same procedure and analysis as she would when writing for television commercials—ask the same questions she would ask when working on television commercials. The objective is to find the most appropriate musical style and obtain the approval of the creatives. Discuss everything in detail before composing and arranging.

PROCEDURE

The script must be analyzed.

Understand the script. The music will not work without the composer having a thorough understanding of the script and the role the creatives want the music to play. Ask the creatives if they can play an example of a musical style that would be appropriate. If not, assemble some examples that would seem appropriate. Play them for the creatives and decide on an acceptable musical style.

Time each section. Break the script down into sections by timings. Determine where the music should change and mark it with detailed notes.

Lay out the score exactly like a television commercial. Decide on a tempo(s) and write down on the score paper or in a music sequencing computer program where musical changes should occur. Since there are no pictures, try to visualize what the pictures would look like if the spot were filmed. Create the pictures through the music.

The "hits" should be determined by the meaning of the words. The music might be even more important to the final success of a radio commercial than it is to a television commercial because there is one less element—there are no pictures. Try to write the music so that visual images are created in the listener's mind.

Determine the tempo(s) and meter(s) of each measure before writing. If this is not done, it is difficult to lay out the score, because the dialogue will not match the measure numbers. When reading the script to a metronome click, the composer can determine if there will be any odd meters within the piece. The score could possibly have a 4/4, 3/4, and a 2/4 bar consecutively and continue with a variety of beats per measure. The goal is to write a piece of music that does not sound disruptive.

RADIO BUDGETS

Radio music budgets are generally lower than television budgets, which generally affects the size of the band and number of vocalists and musicians that can be hired. Problems can result from this. Most radio commercials are expanded versions of television commercials, but the radio budgets might not accommodate the same number of singers and musicians used in the television spots. This must be discussed with the creatives. If this potential problem is discussed before the budget is submitted, the agency may request the same production budget for the radio music so the music will sound the same. If the same budget is not approved, explain to the creatives that the track will not sound the same and try to clarify what the differences will be. The worst thing you can do is to present a "surprise" to the creatives at the session. When dealing with nonmusicians, it is important to be clear when explaining music. They might say they understand your intentions, but when listening to the music at the recording session, the first question they ask is, "Why doesn't it sound the same as the television music?"

The arranger can combine synthesizers with live musicians to help make the track sound more like a version produced using a larger band or orchestra. Even though this technique will certainly help, nothing can replace the sound of live performers. Synthesizers do not provide the individuality and feel of live players.

ANALYSIS

The following is a radio commercial written by the copywriter and submitted to the composer as a worksheet:

Council on Family Health Read the Label Campaign

:60 "Corner"
SFX: Mystery detective music
Announcer (ECHO AS IN AN ALLEYWAY): Psst . . . listen over here. Gotta tell you something . . . when it comes to taking medicine, what you don't know CAN hurt you. Be a know-it-all. Read the medicine label. Hey, it's your body. So, you'd better make it your business to find out everything about everything that goes inside it. The when to—the why to—the don't do—and especially—the never do. Because, sometimes a medicine that works for one person isn't going to work for another. Or, sometimes, certain foods, beverages, or other medicines you take might interfere with how safely and effectively the medicine you take works. Or, you might even have forgotten the right dosage or what hour you're supposed to take it. Or . . . you get the point. So, when it comes to getting better safely and effectively, with no unpleasant surprises inside your body—be a know-it-all and read the label. This message brought to you by the Council on Family Health and the FDA.

To help the writing process, the composer must break down the commercial into timings and indicate the overall feel of the music. The instructions for the following commercial were to make the music light and almost "cartoon-like." Try to internalize a basic musical mood when reading the dialogue.

Use the following commercial as a practice exercise, prerecording the dialogue and using the suggested timings as a guide:

SFX: Mystery detective music
Announcer (ECHO AS IN AN ALLEYWAY):

1. Psst . . .listen over here. Gotta tell you something . . . :04 (approximate timings per section)
2. When it comes to taking medicine, what you don't know CAN hurt you. :05
3. Be a know-it-all. Read the medicine label. :02 1/2
4. Hey, it's your body. So, you'd better make it your business to find out everything about everything that goes inside it. :06
5. The when to—the why to— :02
6. The don't do— :01½
7. And especially—the never do. :02½
8. Because sometimes a medicine that works for one person isn't going to work for another. :05
9. Or, sometimes, certain foods, beverages, or other medicines you take might interfere with how safely and effectively the medicine you take works. :09
10. Or, you might even have forgotten the right dosage or what hour you're suppose to take it. :06
11. Or . . . you get the point. :02
12. So, when it comes to getting better safely and effectively, with no unpleasant surprises inside your body—:06
13. Be a know-it-all and read the label. :03
14. This message brought to you by the Council on Family Health and the FDA :05

Total of :59½

RADIO JINGLES

Radio jingles are usually one minute in length and usually follow the television version of the same campaign (assuming there is a television version). Radio campaigns normally require several arrangements of the basic jingle. As mentioned in chapter 7, make sure that the jingle is adaptable.

There are music houses, mostly located in the smaller markets, that record generic radio and television jingles in almost every style of music. They license the same jingle in different markets for a specified period of time. The music house will include the name of the product in the new lyric. Of course, you might hear the same jingle in one hundred different markets, but for a local advertiser, that doesn't matter. Their customers will most likely never hear the other versions.

The same process is used to sell local news themes and station IDs to various markets. Most station IDs are recorded in Dallas, because Texas is a right-to-work state, and there are no unions. This means the performers don't have to be paid union scale or given residual payments.

CONCLUSION

Writing music for radio has to be approached as a distinctive craft; it differs from writing for television because of the lack of pictures. Always try to compose the music so the audience can visualize the commercial. A good test is to play the music without hearing the dialogue and see if the meaning of the commercial is still conveyed.

If the music is written to "go against the picture" (e.g., writing happy music when it should really be sad), the dialogue must be heard to understand the meaning of the music. This compositional method is used more often in television writing than for radio.

ASSIGNMENT

Assignment

Analyze the following commercial and compose several different pieces. Record the script on a CD or cassette and use it as a reference when composing. Make sure the reading does not exceed :30.

Council on Family Health Read the Label Campaign: "Come to Me"

Hey, it's your body. So, you'd better make it your business to find out everything about everything that goes inside it. When people want to know about the medicine they're taking, they come to me for the answers. Who am I? I tell you when you should take it, if you should take it, how often you should take it, what you should take it with, what you shouldn't take with it. Who am I? The label. Be a know-it-all. Read the label. This message brought to you by the Council on Family Health and the FDA.

Composer's Breakdown

1. Hey, it's your body. So, you'd better make it your business to find out about everything that goes inside it.
2. When people want to know about the medicine they're taking, they come to me for the answers.
3. Who am I?
4. I tell you when you should take it, if you should take it, how often you should take it, what you should take it with, what you shouldn't take with it.
5. Who am I?
6. The label.
7. Be a know-it-all.
8. Read the label.
9. This message brought to you by the Council on Family Health and the FDA.

9

Corporate Videos and Infomercials
(Long-Form Commercials)

More often than not, the music in corporate videos sounds "canned," and, therefore, less effective because of the use of generic stock music. Conversely, music scored for corporate videos can completely change the effect and mood of what is being communicated. The same idea is true for a motion picture, a TV special, or TV commercial; scored music greatly enhances the overall impact of the message it is delivering.

As a producer/director, I cannot allow cost to motivate whether I use original music or not. For me, it is better, and oftentimes more cost effective, to use a talented composer of synthesized music than wasting time and money searching for and securing the rights to stock music.

For me, persuading a group of bankers, insurance brokers, or doctors, through the use of corporate video, is no different than a feature film director's need to stimulate an audience in the local Cineplex. My job is to motivate the viewer to accept and use the product I've been asked by my client to sell; no different, in concept, than a feature film director [who] is asked by his or her producers to "sell" the story that gives credence to that feature film. Original music helps do that.

—Dennis Powers, president, Dennis Powers Productions

CORPORATE VIDEOS

Corporate video is an inclusive term for many genres of videos made for businesses. They include training videos, product videos, and informational videos. Some businesses, like pharmaceutical companies, introduce new products by producing informational corporate videos, which are released to the press as well as to their employees. Some are very detailed and technical. For example, the press will want to know the medical terminology used to describe a new drug. A newspaper columnist or a television reporter has to have enough information to inform the public.

Some salespeople travel with laptop computers and a CD-ROM of a corporate video and use it as a sales tool for prospective clients. Corporate videos are played in department stores to give an in-depth perspective of a product to the potential consumer. It is common to see an exercise video looping (repeating) on a television screen while a nearby salesperson is giving a live demonstration and taking orders. Almost every genre of business uses corporate videos to promote and inform its employees and customers: for example, cruise ship companies, travel agencies, and live industrial shows presented at conventions and corporate meetings.

DIRECTORS

Some film production companies specialize in producing corporate videos. In this case, the composer is generally dealing with either the producer or the director. The videos can run any length. The author has composed music for sixty-minute corporate videos and ten-minute corporate videos.

Unlike with commercials, for corporate videos, the composer is usually brought in after the film or video has been shot. Scoring a corporate video is similar to scoring a television program, except that in the case of the corporate video, something is being "sold." There can be dramatic segments and informational segments within the same production. There is no standardized format. Executives from the marketing department of a corporate client meet with the director and express a definite corporate goal and message they want to communicate with a video. The director then has a script written and submits a first draft. (Many corporate directors write their own scripts.) The script is usually revised until the client gives final approval and "green-lights" the production.

SPOTTING SESSION

The spotting session is when the director or producer views the film with the composer, and they discuss exactly which segments should be scored and the style of music required. These decisions are crucial to the success of the film because an inappropriate style of music can send the wrong message to the viewer and hinder the effectiveness of the film.

> The composer makes a cue sheet, which is a map of each cue. The SMPTE and action that coincides with those numbers are notated. Film composers enjoy the luxury of having music editors make the cue sheets.

The composer is usually asked to send a demonstration reel of her music that is similar in style to the music required for the video. The production company will normally play the reel for the clients and receive their approval to hire the composer. The clients must always approve the musical style and are usually very particular because of the important contribution music plays in shaping the overall affect of the video. The composer must be careful not to offend any of the target audience. Many times, there is a broad range of people watching the video and the music should be appealing to the general audience. If the video is targeted for a certain demographic, then the music must appeal to that audience. It is the same approach that is taken when writing music for commercials.

MUSICAL APPROACH

Since most corporate videos are long-form, the composer has to think of the score as being closer to a television or film score than a commercial. The composer can write a theme and variations or approach each cue as an individual piece, using a compositional device to sew the score together so that it sounds cohesive. The musical approach is always discussed with the producer and/or director, and agreement should always be made concerning what events must be "hit" (accented) and whether the hit should be subtle or direct.

Some videos are produced in segments, with each segment being introduced by a separation banner, for example, "THE OFFICE," "THE FACTORY." The composer might suggest that each segment card be on the screen for the same number of seconds and a logo-style piece of music repeated for each card. This helps to create unity within the score.

> There are instances where music is not appropriate. The author scored music for a pharmaceutical product that could help paraplegics. In some segments of the video, the director did not want to include music, because it was more dramatic leaving it out.

Some corporate videos have elaborate openings that require a piece of music that is closer to the style of music that might be used for a commercial than to the music composed for the remainder of the score. Some contain animated corporate logos that immediately create an image for the company. Sometimes, a revision of the opening is used in the closing and should be scored with a similar arrangement.

BUDGET

Because most corporate videos have low budgets, the majority of the scores are synthesized. If a large company is producing an elaborate video, for example, for a corporate meeting, the budget might include enough to hire a small orchestra. The producer will generally offer the composer an all-inclusive budget. There is very little negotiating with corporate videos. The music budget is generally the first to be eliminated or reduced. In fact many directors use stock music instead of original scores. Most important videos have original scores because directors want the music to match each scene and not just sound like a nondescript bed of mood music.

The following is my interview with Dennis Powers, director and writer of corporate videos:

Question: "What is a corporate video?"

Dennis: "There are many kinds of corporate videos . . . generally speaking, a corporate video outlines or describes what it is about a corporation that makes it unique . . . makes it special . . . makes it different. It describes the corporation and gives the viewer a feeling for what the corporation does . . . who the people who run the corporation, and what the talent pool is like that makes the corporation run. These are definitions that are sort of general, but that's mostly the kind of work that I do. There are other corporate videos that are more specific and targeted to different audiences, depending on what the corporation does. Pfizer, for instance, will do videos for certain divisions that explain or describe a certain product. Sometimes those corporate videos go out to people who sell the products or go out to doctors, for instance, and then there are other corporate videos that are strategic and slightly more cerebral that kind of give more of a sense of what a corporation is about. It doesn't have to be specific information, but it can be more like a mood or a feeling or an essence of what a corporation stands for."

Question: "How does working on a corporate video differ from working on a commercial?"

Dennis: "A corporate video, just by the nature of being longer, has more information. It's like taking a commercial and stretching it out, but, I treat it pretty much the same way as I would treat a commercial. I think that the shooting and editing [of the film] and [scoring] the music are all inherently important . . . the way I treat corporate videos, because of my background in commercials, would be to look at a subject, to delineate what that subject is, and then to fine-line certain aspects of it . . . almost like treating it as individual commercials. So, I think you have the luxury in a corporate video of telling more stories, of getting into personalities within the corporation, or developing characters in a way, like you would in a movie."

Question: "How often are corporate videos made for in-house use?"

Dennis: "Probably about 50 percent of what I do remains in-house—[the purpose is] to motivate employees—to give specific information that the upper management wants them to understand more thoroughly. About 50 percent [of my videos] goes to the outside [for other purposes]." (Dennis produced several videos of the Boys Club of Harlem playing basketball in China and in Cuba.)

Question: "Do you consider the videos you produced for the Boys Club corporate videos?"

Dennis: "They're principally used for fund-raising. The Boys Club pieces, both the Beijing, the China piece, and the Cuba piece, are essentially to inform the public that the Boys Club wants to reach out . . . so that's the workhorse. . . .they take these videos around to various schools that they are trying to get Boys Club kids into . . . prep schools, particularly on the East coast, to show the kinds of things that the Boys Club is doing . . . but it's motivational and fund-raising more than anything else . . . in this context, it's more documentary in nature, and through storytelling in documentary fashion, you can get people involved, and they kind of get the feeling of what you are doing, and it becomes motivational, and the motivation, of course, becomes one of financial gift giving."

(This interview shows that music for corporate videos is a hybrid between scoring commercials and scoring documentaries. It provides the composer with an opportunity to be creative more in the way a film composer is, primarily because it is long-form.)

INFOMERCIALS

Infomercials are long-form commercials that usually run either thirty or sixty minutes, which is the length of a full television program. (Infomercials are also played on the radio, but less frequently than on television.) They are advertisements! *Infomercials are designed to get immediate consumer response*—a toll-free number is promoted throughout the program, which the customer can call to order the product.

Another form of infomercial is called DRTV, which means Direct Response Television. Most DRTV spots run one or two minutes but are sometimes longer or shorter. Like long-form infomercials, they require a direct response from the audience.

Although infomercials are strictly designed to result in immediate phone or Internet sales, surveys have shown a direct correlation between the showing of infomercials and increased sales in retail stores.

AIRTIME

Since most infomercials are shown at unusual hours—mostly after midnight—this presents an opportunity to buy viewing time at inexpensive rates. Media companies buy bulk time and resell it to infomercial companies. Both cable and broadcasting time is available, but the majority of the bulk time is on cable channels.

A survey showed that 15 percent of all televisions are on at 1:00 A.M. and more than 66 percent of cable TV viewers surf the channels. This presents an opportunity for the viewers to watch an infomercial. Sometimes it is difficult to tell when a program is an infomercial until the hard sell occurs. Many celebrities have very successfully promoted products in infomercials and are paid with a percentage of sales. A successful infomercial can generate millions of dollars. Having said this, I must point out that most infomercials lose money. Infomercials are usually tested in a region over one or two weekends. If the sales are not good, the infomercial is not run again.

The following list contains some of the most successful infomercials:

1. Jane Fonda: Fitness Trends for the Nineties (treadmill)
2. Psychic Friends Network (1-900 line)
3. Bruce Jenner: PowerWalk Plus (treadmill)
4. Connie Sellecca and John Tesh: Growing in Love and Hidden Keys
5. Jake Steinfeld: Body by Jake (hip and thigh exercise machine)
6. Barbara De Angelis: Making Love Work
7. Health Rider (fitness machine)
8. Popeil Pasta Maker
9. Anthony Robbins: Personal Power #4 (self-improvement)

Here is my interview with Mark Mayhew, of Mayhew/Breen Production, one of the most successful infomercial producers:

Question: "What is an infomercial?"

Mark: "An infomercial is a twenty-eight minute and thirty second broadcast piece that is used to sell a product or to convey information about a product."

Question: "Other than the length, how does an infomercial differ from a commercial?"

Mark: "A commercial is designed to enhance the image of a product and create an awareness that can be acted on later on, whether it's in a store or in some other way. An infomercial demands a direct response—thus the name 'direct response.' [The audience] calls for information about a product at that moment or actually buys something."

Question: "What is the role of music in an infomercial?"

Mark: "[It] is not unlike its role in a commercial, but in an infomercial we use music to enhance the need to buy. We have one of the most difficult jobs, and that is to get people up off their comfortable seat and get to a phone and take down a number. We use music to enhance that need. We use it to help us drive the sale."

Question: "Is creating an infomercial different from creating a commercial?"

Mark: "It's not fundamentally different, in that you're working on a product for which you're creating an image. In traditional advertising, that image does not have to be acted upon in that minute. In our business, we're still creating an image for the product, but we hope to get direct response. The function of music is identical, in that it has to enhance the message in what we're trying to do."

Question: "Is scoring an infomercial closer to scoring a television program than scoring a commercial?"

Mark: "It is much closer to doing a television show. I think that the whole process of the infomercial is much closer to a television program than it is to image advertising. In order to keep someone involved for half an hour, you have to tell them a story that is interesting, you have to repeat the story in different ways, you have to convey your information."

Question: "So most of the composers who work on commercials also compose music for infomercials?"

Mark: "I would say, probably, yes. I don't really know people who [just compose for infomercials]."

Question: "Are you hired by advertising companies?"

Mark: "We are almost never hired by [an] advertising agency. We are mostly hired by marketing companies—occasionally, we will work with an advertising agency that has been asked to do an infomercial and doesn't want to touch it. On occasion, we are hired by a wealthy entrepreneur who wants to do something on his own."

Question: "What does it take to warrant keeping an infomercial on the air?"

Mark: "It takes sales that are able to comfortably cover the cost of media plus the cost of the production of the item. For instance, if you spend your thousand dollars to buy your half-hour, and you make a thousand dollars, most likely you're going to go out of business very quickly, because you're not covering any of the additional cost. You may have covered the cost of media time, but you haven't covered the cost of the infomercial, the manufacturing for the infomercial, and all of the prototype work."

Question: "What percentage of infomercials make money?"

Mark: "Maybe one out of twenty-five."

Question: "Do you find that most of the products are tested before spending the money to make and promote an infomercial?"

Mark: "Not necessarily—it's a high-risk, high-return business."

Question: "What are some of the infomercials that you have produced?"

Mark: "In fitness we have done Body by Jake, Cable Flex with Jackie Chan, Ab-Flex, Fast Track with Cathy Rigby—we've done shows for Quaker State Motor Oil, Bayliner Boats, and Bose Speakers, with Herbie Hancock.

MUSIC FOR INFOMERCIALS

Infomercials present an interesting challenge to the composer. It is like composing music for a television show, including the commercials. The format of most infomercials includes a host(s) who makes the audience feel comfortable. Most viewers do not realize they are watching a long-form commercial until the call to action (CTA). The CTA is the actual commercial—hard sell—that occurs frequently within the infomercial. During these sections the audience is expected to pick up the telephone and order the product. Many production companies spend a majority of the budget producing these sections. Some sections might be animated to help show what the product can do. If the CTAs are not well constructed, the product will generally not sell. The CTAs always include a toll-free telephone number, the features of the product, the price, credit card or check information, and the address. Most of them boast a guaranteed return policy within a certain time frame.

Before the CTAs there are usually numerous testimonials from satisfied customers. The testimonials are usually scattered throughout the entire program and can be very effective in generating sales.

APPROACHING THE SCORE

Spot the Film

The first step is to spot the film along with the director or producer. The style of music and purpose of the music must be discussed in detail. Most infomercials have noninvasive scores because the director does not want any attention taken away from the program. He generally wants the music to create an overall mood. The director will usually tell the composer where the music should be more demonstrative. This generally occurs during the call-to-action sequences. Since this is truly a commercial within the commercial, these sections are sometimes scored like a commercial. Infomercials vary in style, and the composer should not assume that the approach to every infomercial is the same. All of the pertinent questions that the composer would ask the creatives when doing a commercial should also be asked of the infomercial director.

Bumpers

Bumpers are short pieces of music that separate sections within the video. Bumper music in an infomercial is usually the same piece of music repeated each time there is a section change. Sometimes the length of the bumper will vary, but the basic music remains the same. Bumpers are used in television programs before going to a commercial break and also to reenter the program. A well-designed, catchy bumper can create a signature sound. [Listen to track #11 on the enclosed CD.]

Testimonials

Testimonials by satisfied customers are always an important part of an infomercial. Some directors want the same basic music for each testimonial. Sometimes the arrangement and length might vary but the basic theme for those sections remains the same. This is the same theory that is used for the bumper music—it creates an identity.

Opening Theme

Create an identifiable theme for the opening. Some directors want the composer to develop the score from this theme—to create a theme and variations. This approach is commonly used in film scoring. If the composer decides to use this approach, get approval from the director first.

Video Game Music

Music for video games has become a great source of income for composers. There are many music companies that only produce scores for video games.

The music has become very complex and time consuming to compose. Although the main genre of music is sound design, songs are also used. When video games first appeared, the makers of the games supplied cute little tunes to go along with the games. As technology advanced, so did the need for well-crafted music and professional production. Many film and commercial composers score video games. Some scores have become so popular that the music is released on commercial CDs. One video game, in Japan, spawned a hit record.

CONCLUSION

The composer must try to compose a cohesive score rather than just individual cues that are not related. Approach an infomercial or corporate video more like a film score than a commercial, but always be aware that the purpose of the film/video is to sell or inform—not necessarily to entertain. (Some music companies specialize in composing music for infomercials, and other companies specialize in corporate videos.)

ASSIGNMENTS

1. Watch several infomercials on television; compare the way the program is formatted with the placement and use of music.
2. Watch and analyze some corporate videos.

10

The Business of Commercials

It is necessary for anyone associated with music for commercials to understand the basics of the *business* of commercials. Even though the primary focus of this book is the creative process, an overview of the business is necessary.

In the United States, the hubs for national advertising are located in New York, Los Angeles, Chicago, and Nashville. Most professionals working in commercial music in these locations belong to unions (which will be discussed in this chapter), and instrumentalists and singers receive residual payments for their work. Residual payments are additional payments to musicians and singers based on the length of time a commercial is played and the number of regions it is played in. The various unions have dissimilar payment scales, which are periodically renegotiated with representatives of the advertising industry.

> Composers do *not* receive residuals. Over the years composers have unsuccessfully tried to negotiate for this benefit. To compensate for the loss of this potential income, some companies charge large creative fees.
>
> Composers who write for music houses will almost always be included on the musicians' and singers' contracts, so they can be paid session fees and residuals.

MARKETING A MUSIC COMPANY

Reels to Demonstrate Work

Music houses or individual composers always have an audio reel(s) and a video reel(s) that serve as a demonstration of their work. It is advisable that reels do not run more than seven to ten minutes each.

When an agency producer requests a reel, the producer will usually be very specific about the kind of music he is looking for. Try to customize the reel for each individual request. It is difficult to be selected for a job without showing a piece of music that is almost exactly like the kind of music the agency is looking for. Usually three or four examples on a separate reel are sufficient. If the agency is not familiar with the composer's work, the composer should also include a general reel.

> It is advisable to keep a music library that is filed by category, for example, jazz, jingles, rock and roll, rhythm and blues, and so on. There can also be subgenres, for example, male rock and roll vocals, light female vocals, and so on. Make it easy to find any example that may be requested. Some music companies have a number of reels that are divided into categories. They may have a children's reel, a world music reel, a jingle reel, and so on. Update the reels as often as possible.
>
> All singers have demo reels. Collect reels of the best singers and keep them filed by category. When working on jingles, the creatives will want to hear a reel of the lead singer. It is advisable to submit several reels and let them choose their favorite. If they do not like a singer at the session, they will request a new singer, and the music company will generally incur the additional expense.

Image

Many music companies and individual composers create an image based on their strong points. Some, for example, specialize in jingles, others in underscoring and sound design. Always market the strongest work. One should never accept a job that one does not feel comfortable with. Nobody is fully versatile.

Follow through with business cards, stationery, and a website that depicts the image of the company. Some of the websites enable the viewer to play both video and audio samples of their commercials. They also provide a complete background of the music company and each composer and jingle writer. A well-built website can create a company image.

Representatives

Most jingle houses and some individual composers have representatives, called reps. Their job is to approach advertising agencies in a sales capacity. They meet with agency people and develop relationships that it is hoped will lead to work.

A typical meeting would include playing the most recent video and audio sample reels. The objective is to find out when the agency will need the services of a music company and the style of music they will be in search of. Agencies usually know their shooting schedules several months in advance and will sometimes make the information available. A creative rep will have the music house assemble a special reel with music that they feel will be appropriate for the upcoming commercial. They will send the reel to the agency producer with a note explaining the purpose of the reel. The producer may use some of the music on a temp track when editing the spot. This can sometimes lead to the music company's receiving the final assignment.

In some music companies, the reps negotiate the fees and calculate the budgets. The job varies from company to company. It is often advisable to have the rep at the recording session to "hand-hold" the agency creatives and to be the intermediary between the agency and the music company. Sessions can become unruly when there are too many chefs in the kitchen. It is wise for one person from the music company to deal with the agency people and relay their opinions and suggestions to the composer or arranger.

Fliers and Newsletters

Some music companies send out fliers and newsletters (generally through e-mail) updating agencies on their current activities. This helps to create awareness and to keep the company's activities current with producers and the creatives.

> Marketing ideas are merely aids to draw attention to the music company. The only parameter that will eventually get the work is musical excellence. The best marketing aid is to have diverse video and audio reels that show inventive and competent work. It is also important to complete projects on schedule and to conduct the entire business in a professional manner. Advertising music is a business and must be conducted as such to retain clients. '

Ads

Some companies take out ads in trade magazines. Most often those ads focus on their latest commercials, and they try to project a company image. Some companies specialize in certain musical styles, while others claim to have enough composers and jingle writers to be a full-service music house. The company should always focus on its strengths.

> Ironically (according to music company representatives whom the author has spoken with), advertising music houses have not generally been effective. The consensus from these companies is that advertising has rarely resulted in direct sales but has resulted in awareness of the companies, which has helped to open new relationships.

Public Relations Firms

Some companies hire public relations firms. It is their job to have articles published about the music company and to obtain as much publicity as possible. The best exposure is in trade magazines like *Advertising Age*. Trade magazines publish the names of the suppliers connected with a particular commercial. For example, it will list the product, the advertising agency and producer, the copywriter, the art director, the editor, the composer, the music company, and the director and the name of the director's company. This information is usually published weekly. Other potential employers see this information and then contact suppliers they might be interested in. Word of mouth results from public relations.

Company Bio

Have a short bio of the music company, which should contain a list of previous clients. This serves as a good introduction to a potential client. Include it when sending out demonstration reels.

TRADEMARK PROTECTION

A trademark is a symbol or a name that identifies a company or manufacturer and is registered as a form of protection. Music houses sometimes will trademark the name and symbol (called a logo) of their company. After establishing an image, they want their image protected so other companies cannot use their trademark and capitalize on their image.

The application process takes about eighteen months. Information and forms can be found on the Internet at www.uspto.gov. Some attorneys specialize in clearing trademarks. Since there can be complications, it is best to use a specialist.

Some trademarks are extremely valuable. For example, the Coke trademark is worth sixty-nine billion dollars (the shape of their bottle is trademarked, among other things); the Disney trademark is worth thirty-two billion. This is not to say that a music house will have the same value, but after spending time and money to establish an image it is best to be protected.

DEALING WITH THE AGENCY

When discussing business, the rep normally deals with the agency producer. The producer will generally request a detailed budget from the music company. Sometimes, the agency has a predetermined gross musical budget and will ask the music company to break it down. When the music house submits a budget, there is generally some negotiating until a mutually acceptable budget is agreed upon. The agency will then draw a detailed agreement spelling out the exact terms of the entire job. The music company must sign the agreement before the work begins. This is important for both sides, because if there is a dispute, everything is documented in the agreement.

> This is the time to fight for the best budget possible. If the budget is too low to accomplish the creative objectives of the agency, let them know. Once a budget has been approved, it is very difficult to have additional funds allocated to the project.
>
> Tell the creatives that for budget A, you can produce a track that will not contain certain elements (e.g., real strings as opposed to synthesized strings), but for budget B you can accomplished the job in the manner in which the job has been creatively conceived.

Most often there will be a satisfactory compromise. Always make the agency feel that no matter what the budget is, you will produce a suitable track—it just might need some adjustments.

Sometimes music companies will negotiate a total price for the job and not be required to submit a detailed budget. If there are residuals, the agency will have to know the number of musicians and singers in order to calculate the residual payments. If there are no residuals, it is usually not necessary to submit a budget.

BUDGET

The budget below is based on areas of the country where membership in unions is mandatory in order to work. The agency and client must know how many musicians and singers will be on the contract so they can estimate how much the residual payments will be. These payments are included in the agencies' overall budget that has to be approved by the client.

> Traditionally, advertising agencies add a commission that is over and above the production costs (an average is 15 percent). In more recent times, the agencies receive fees instead of a percentage. The agency's compensation is always negotiable.
>
> Some large clients require that at least three qualified companies bid on each line item of the production budget, that is, music, director, and so on. If all of the suppliers are of equal creative ability, the lowest bid will get the job.

RIGHT-TO-WORK STATES

There are some states that do not require union membership. If a nonunion musician or singer works on a union job, the law requires them to be paid the same scale as the union members. In reality, in most states that are right-to-work, the unions are very weak, and most music companies negotiate buyout fees. This means that one fee covers the entire production. The music company then negotiates individual fees for each musician, singer, composer, and/or arranger, which are deducted from their overall fee.

In the United States the majority of nonunion work is created in Dallas, Texas. Most radio identification jingles and a substantial amount of music for commercials are recorded for regional and local advertising in Dallas, because there are no residual payments. The client can use the music for a negotiated period of time; sometimes they buy the rights in perpetuity.

For recording in a right-to-work state, the overall cost is usually less than that for recording in a major market. The fees are based on the size of the market—larger markets warrant higher creative fees.

MUSIC BUDGET

Most music companies pay their composers and arrangers based on a percentage of the creative fees received by the music company. For example, a composer or arranger might receive from one-third to 40 percent of what the music company receives as a creative or arranging fee.

The music company usually separates the portion of the budget that deals with studio charges because it is not considered part of the creative fee. When there is a rep (agent for the music company), his or her commission is also deducted before arriving at the net creative fee.

> Some music companies have large overheads. They might have two or three studios and the equipment is costly. In addition, they have to pay studio personnel, accountants, lawyers, and all other normal business services. The music company has to make a profit and will therefore charge a percentage of the overall gross amount received before arriving at fees that will be shared. After those charges are deducted, they arrive at net percentages that form a basis for determining the creative and arranging fees.
>
> Even individual composers have large expenses, because they have to continually upgrade their equipment. Most computers have to be upgraded every two years. New software and hardware, which include synthesizers and effects units, are continually coming on the market. To keep current, these investments must be made.

Demo Fee

The demo is always the first step in the creative process. Most music companies will submit several demos, but they are usually only paid for one. If there are several commercials that require different scores, there is a demo fee for each. A demo budget is usually not included when calculating the final budget. Sometimes, demo fees are deducted from the final budget of the company that is chosen to do the final production.

> Demos are not demos anymore! This means that demos sound like finished productions. In fact some demos go on the air as the final commercial.
> The main gripe heard from music companies is that the demo fees are too low for the amount of work that has to be done. The music company almost always loses money on demos. In essence, the music company is paying to compete. It is willing to accept this because the financial rewards can be substantial if it wins the commercial.
> There is almost always competition. Some music houses develop very close relationships with creatives and agencies and are sometimes rewarded with jobs without having to compete. They still have to satisfy the creatives and the client with the quality of their work, or other companies will be hired to compete. Note: It is industry standard that if a demo is rejected the music company retains the rights. To be safe, make sure that this is stated in the agreement.

Creative Fee

This is a negotiable fee that is paid for an original composition. Fees for high-profile, successful composers are usually higher than fees for composers with less commercial success. Most of the time music companies will not be excessive with their fees because of the potential income from residuals. (Residuals only apply to union jobs.)

Sometimes creative fees are paid in stages. If there is a possibility that the commercial will be played nationally, the agency will sometimes test the commercial in a region first. There might be one fee for a testing period, with the remainder of the fee to be paid when the testing period has ended and the agency begins running the commercial. There are also additional fees when the commercials play out of the United States.

Arranging Fee

The agency might only require an arrangement(s) of an existing piece of music. The agency either owns the music or licenses permission to rearrange existing music, for example, a popular song. If this is the case, there is no creative fee. The music company charges an arranging fee, but sometimes includes a production fee, which equals about one-half of the arranging fee. (Production fees are not considered standard and must be negotiated.)

There is a union scale for arrangements. It is based on the number of measures and the size of the orchestra or combo. Most competent arrangers receive substantially more than union scale. The union only requires that the arranger receive scale on the musician's contract. The remainder of the fee is paid by the music company and should be included in the budget.

> Only union scale is included on the contract because the agencies want to pay the minimum amount of pension and health benefits. If the arranger's fee is higher than union scale, he or she submits an additional bill to the music company. These benefits are based on a percentage of the fee the arranger receives—the higher the fee, the more the cost of pension and health benefits.

If the music company is also responsible for the original composition, it will usually try to negotiate a clause in the agreement that says that the music company must do any additional arrangements of that piece of music. This is a very difficult concession to get.

Costs of Musicians

The musicians receive union scale for each recording session. (Some musicians will not work for less than double scale.)

1. If musicians overdub the same part or add parts, additional payments are due.
2. If a musician plays more than one instrument (called doubling), there is an additional payment due.

3. Health and pension benefits must be included as part of the total budget. This is based on a percentage of each person's wages.
4. An arranger or orchestrator is always budgeted at double scale.
5. If there is a music copyist, the union scale is based on the number of measures and number parts copied.
6. If there is a possibility of overtime, estimate as closely as possible and include it in the budget.
7. Musicians who play a large instrument, for example, a harp or double bass, are entitled to cartage fees in order to transport their instruments. These fees are listed in the American Federation of Musicians (AFM) union agreement.
8. If there are more than a certain number of musicians, the union requires that a contractor be paid. A contractor hires the musicians and usually fills out the union contract. The contractor receives double scale.
9. There is always a leader who receives double scale.
10. If there is a conductor, the conductor receives double scale.

The unions continually negotiate contracts, so always be aware of the most recent scales.

When dealing with nonunion jobs, always let the performers know exactly what is expected of them for a predetermined fee; for example, singers must triple their parts, a clarinet player is also expected to double on the flute. Even though the payments are not based on a union scale, the performers are not going to perform unlimited services for one fee unless it is agreed upon prior to the recording session.

Number of Singers and Cost

Break this down into lead singer(s) and background singers. If the singers overdub their parts or add parts, there are additional payments due. Health and pension benefits must be included in the budget.

Cost of Engineer

Most recording engineers charge by the hour. Sometimes they will agree to a fee for the project as long as there are a maximum number of hours allocated before they receive additional compensation.

Studio Costs

Studio costs include studio time, tape or use of hard disc recording devices, and use of video equipment.

Studio time is charged on an hourly basis. Make certain to include tax in the budget. Always estimate more studio time than needed, because creatives tend to change things during sessions, which can be time consuming.

Fees for Celebrities

If a celebrity is hired to sing or play on a commercial, his or her fees can be very high. The agency negotiates the fees directly with their agent or manager. This is not included in the budget given by the music house.

Instrument Rentals

Sometimes there is a need to rent instruments. Often they are unusual instruments that most players would not own or very large instruments like timpani, boo bams (percussion instrument), or balaphone (African xylophone). Call an instrument rental company and ask prices so they can be included in the budget. If the arranger decides to use additional instruments after the budget has been submitted, take the cost out of the miscellaneous part of the budget.

Most large studios will rent the equipment (as a courtesy to the music house) and charge it on the studio bill. Consult with the instrumentalist before renting an instrument. He might request a specific brand.

Payroll Companies

Handling fees (for talent and residuals) are included in most budgets. Sometimes the music company receives this fee, but most often, outside companies that specialize in performing this service handle the payments. Handling fees can include the preparation of union contracts, the issuing of checks to the performers, the preparation of residual estimates, the preparation of budget estimates, in addition to other services that might be required. Whoever performs this function also handles payments for music companies or agencies. For this service they receive a handling fee, which is based on a percentage of the budget. Include the handling fee in the overall budget. (Sometimes this service is not needed.)

> If the music house is required to pay the talent, make certain to receive the payment in advance. There can be some problems when dealing with small agencies if this is not arranged beforehand. Refuse to do the job until payment is received, because the music company will be held responsible.

Most agencies will submit a short contract, also called a Heads-of-Agreement letter, stating the agreed-upon terms of the job. Make certain that the agreement is very specific; if not, the music supplier could be responsible for payments that were not considered in the basic negotiations. For example, if a jingle is being recorded and the agency changes *one* lyric (word) at the end of a session, overtime might occur. The music company should not be charged for the overtime fee, because the lyric change was not anticipated prior to the recording.

Always state the number of commercials and, in the case of jingles, the number of lyrics to be recorded (even if the backing track remains the same for each lyric). Even if one line of a lyric is changed, it is considered an additional version of the commercial (e.g., a city name, such as "In San Antonio" instead of "In Los Angeles," as stated in a prior version), and the singers must be paid for an additional commercial.

The musicians' union (American Federation of Musicians, or AFM) allows a certain number of commercials to be recorded in one recording session, so there might not be an additional session payment due, but when the commercial plays, it is listed as a separate commercial, which allows the musicians to receive residual payments for each commercial.

The rules for SAG (the Screen Actors Guild is the singer's union used for work in television) are different from those for the AFM (musicians). Singers are paid for each commercial that they sing.

Since union contracts change, always be aware of the most recent revisions.

Most large agencies will ask the music house to supply completed union contracts. The agency will then pay the contract. Check the bylaws of each union to see how quickly the contract must be paid. There are late fees applicable if payment is not made within the time frame stated in the union contract. If the music house does not submit the contracts in a timely manner to the agency, they will be responsible for the late fees—not the agency. (The agency will deduct the late fees from the final payment to the music company.)

The unions require that all performers hired for a recording session be in good standing. This means they have paid their dues and there are no surrounding problems with their eligibility to perform. The agency or music company can be fined if they do not check each individual's status prior to the recording session.

The unions require that the date of the recording session be reported to the union prior to the session. The information required by the unions is the name of the advertising agency, the product name, and the date that the session will occur. If the session is not reported, the unions will (sometimes) fine the music company.

THE UNIONS: SAG, AFTRA, AND AFM

Music houses in major territories must be signatories to certain unions, or they cannot contract musicians and singers.

1. Some states require union membership for a performer to accept union jobs.
2. If a performer is in a union, he or she may not accept nonunion jobs, under any circumstances, without prior permission. For example, the unions might allow performers to work on public service commercials without receiving union scale.
3. Some states, called right-to-work states, do not require union membership. Know the laws of the state you are working in.
4. When dealing with unions, know the laws of that union and follow them exactly as stated—there are large fines for not complying with the rules.

Unions in the United States

The following information deals with the unions and procedures in the United States. Contact each organization or go to its website to gain in-depth information.

There are similar unions and performing rights organizations in other countries. It behooves a music person to become familiar with the organizations and unions in their country.

Unions and Performing Rights Societies

What follows is a general overview of the main organizations and unions that directly affect composers, singers, actors, and announcers (performers) when participating in television and radio commercials.

> Sometimes it is difficult to know which union governs a specific job. There may be two unions involved with one job, for example, a television commercial and a radio commercial require separate contracts with different unions. The scales and bylaws of the unions are not the same.
>
> When something is questionable, call one of the unions for information.

Screen Actors Guild (SAG)

The following information was taken from the SAG website: http://www.sag.org/.

The Screen Actors Guild is a labor union affiliated with the AFL-CIO through the Associated Actors and Artists of America. Singers in major markets must join SAG in order to be eligible to perform on commercials. (SAG is not a union for composers or musicians.)

All singers and instrumentalists who act or appear on-screen in commercials, music videos, television programs, industrial films, and films must be members of SAG.

Union-scale payments are different for singers. The rates are based on being a soloist, a duo, or group singers of three or more. Doubling parts increases the payment. They receive residual payment (extended use) on a per-play basis, as compared with the AFM (musicians) reuse fees, which are based on thirteen-week cycles.

DEFINITIONS (from the Screen Actors Guild)

The Producers signatory hereto and the Union confirm their mutual understanding and agreement that the term "commercials" as used herein and in all prior agreements between the parties, means and includes, and has always meant and included, motion pictures whether made on or by film, tape or otherwise and whether produced by means of motion picture cameras, electronic cameras or devices, tape devices or any combination of the foregoing, or any other means, methods or devices now used or which may hereafter be adopted. The foregoing provision shall be binding upon advertising agencies signatory hereto or to Letters of Adherence referred to in Section 56, Letters of Adherence, except only with respect to commercials made by means of electronic tape or any other electronic device produced for such advertising agencies by television stations or television networks using broadcasting studio facilities of such television stations or television networks.

Commercials are short advertising or commercial messages made as motion pictures, 3 minutes or less in length, and intended for showing over television. Advertising or commercial messages include any narration, dialogue, songs, jingles or other matter which depict or mention the advertiser's name, product or service. They include program openings and closings which mention the advertiser's name, product or service. Advertising and commercial messages over 3 minutes in length shall be subject to separate negotiations between the Union and Producer.

The term "commercials" also includes short advertising messages intended for showing on the Internet which would be treated as commercials if broadcast on television and which are capable of being used on television in the same form as on the Internet. If a dispute arises as to whether material used on the Internet qualifies as a commercial, as defined above, either party may submit the dispute to a joint committee established by the Joint Policy Committee and the Union. The joint committee shall consist of an equal number of persons appointed by the Joint Policy Committee and by the Union. If the joint committee fails to resolve the dispute within thirty days, either party may submit the dispute to arbitration.

MISSION STATEMENT OF SCREEN ACTORS GUILD

The Screen Actors Guild represents its members through:

Negotiation and enforcement of collective bargaining agreements which establish equitable levels of compensation, benefits, and working conditions for performers;

The collection of compensation for exploitation of their recorded performances and protection against unauthorized use; and the preservation and expansion of work opportunities.

JOINING QUALIFICATIONS

A performer may become eligible for Screen Actors Guild membership under one of the following conditions:

1) PROOF OF SAG EMPLOYMENT

A. Principal Performer Employment: Performers may join SAG upon proof of employment or prospective employment within two weeks or less by a SAG signatory company. Employment must be in a principal or speaking role in a SAG film, videotape, television program or commercial. Proof of such employment may be in the form of a signed contract, a payroll check or check stub, or a letter from the company (on company letterhead) The document proving employment must provide the following information: applicant's name and Social Security number, the name of the production or the commercial (the product name), the salary paid in dollar amount, and the specific date(s) worked.

B. Background Players Employment: Performers may join SAG upon proof of employment as a SAG covered background player at full SAG rates and conditions for a MINIMUM of three workdays subsequent to March 25, 1990. Employment must be by a company signed to a SAG Background Players Agreement, and in a SAG film, videotape, television program or commercial. Proof of such employment must be in the form of a signed employment voucher (or time card), plus an original payroll check or check stub. Such documents must provide the same information listed in paragraph 1)A above.

The American Federation of Television and Radio Artists (AFTRA)

The following information was taken from the AFTRA website (http://aftra.com):

AFTRA represents actors and other professional performers, and broadcasters in live and taped television, radio, sound recordings, non-broadcast/industrial programming, and new technologies such as interactive programming and CD-ROMs. AFTRA is used most often for singers working on radio commercials.

When a performer accepts their first union job, they are able to perform without joining the union. The performer must then become a union member within thirty days following that job in order to participate in the next union job. Members pay an initiation fee plus yearly dues. The dues are calculated on the gross earnings of the individual performer. AFTRA provides a pension plan plus other benefits.

Residual payments (reuse payments) are based on per-use payments. This means that each time the spot plays the singers receive additional payments. The reuse fees are based on a very complicated formula, which is based on a geographical formula and how frequently the spot plays. The only way to project residual payment is to know what the media buy is.

AFTRA is a labor union and affiliated with the AFL-CIO.

The American Federation of Musicians of the United States and Canada (AFM)

The following information is quoted from the AFM website (http://www.afm.org):

With over 250 local unions throughout the United States and Canada, we are the largest union in the world, representing the interests of professional musicians.

The union represents musicians, contractors, music copyists, arrangers, orchestrators, vocalists, and conductors. Members file contracts for records, film, television and videotape, broadcast television, cable television, pay television, television and radio commercials, live events, industrial films, and other organized events. Except for the Commercial Announcements Agreement, there are no standard rates for the Internet as of yet. It is an all-inclusive union.

The AFM has local offices throughout the United States and Canada and an international office located in New York City. Local offices handle all work within their jurisdiction but are governed by the rules of the national office. Union scale (minimum payment) differs depending on the type of work and the area of the country.

Members pay an initiation fee to join the union and then pay yearly dues plus work dues, which are based on a percentage of each payment received through the union. A percentage of all monies collected goes to the international office. For work performed under the Commercial Announcements Agreement, additional payments are due every 13-week cycle for the life of the commercial. Sometimes the same music used on the original spot(s) is dubbed into new commercials. In this event, each musician on the original session is entitled to additional payments.

Members receive pension benefits and are able to participate in additional benefits if they choose.

The AFM is affiliated with the AFL-CIO.

BMI, ASCAP, AND SEASAC ARE PERFORMING RIGHTS ORGANIZATIONS

There is performance income (airplay) generated by the airplay of a commercial. Some agencies let composers collect performance income, and others do not. Most advertising agencies keep the publishing rights to anything written for the agency; the writer's contracts are work-for-hire contracts, which means the composer gives up all rights to the agency.

Broadcast Music Incorporated (BMI)

The following information is a direct quotation from the BMI website (http://www.bmi.com/home.asp):

BMI is an American performing rights organization that represents approximately 300,000 songwriters, composers and music publishers in all genres of music. The non-profit-making company, founded in 1940, collects license fees on behalf of those American creators it represents, as well as thousands of creators from around the world who chose BMI for representation in the United States. The license fees BMI collects for the "public performances" of its repertoire of approximately 4.5 million compositions—including radio airplay, broadcast and cable television carriage, Internet and live and recorded performances by all other users of music—are then distributed as royalties to the writers, composers and copyright holders it represents.

If a composer of a commercial belongs to BMI, and the agency/client is willing to pay performance royalties, the commercial must be registered with BMI. BMI will then collect and distribute the performance royalty income.

The American Society of Composers, Authors and Publishers (ASCAP)

The following is a direct quotation from the ASCAP website (http://ascap.com/index.html):

ASCAP is a membership association of more than 120,000 U.S. composers, songwriters and publishers of every kind of music and hundreds of thousands worldwide. ASCAP is the only U.S. performing rights organization created and controlled by composers, songwriters and music publishers, with a Board of Directors elected by and from the membership.

ASCAP protects the rights of its members by licensing and distributing royalties for the non-dramatic public performances of their copyrighted works. ASCAP's licensees encompass all who want to perform copyrighted music publicly. ASCAP makes giving and obtaining permission to perform music simple for both creators and users of music.

Work for Hire

Most agencies require composers or music houses to sign a work-for-hire agreement. This means that the agency owns the composition or arrangement in perpetuity and the composer has no claims to the music or arrangement. Unfortunately, when dealing with a large agency this is a standard clause. Some small agencies will allow the composer to keep the rights mainly because the creative fee might be below a standard fee and this becomes a form of compensation. Some agencies will allow composers to collect performance royalties; this is a point of negotiation and is worth asking for.

Synchronization Licenses

A synchronization license (also called a sync license) is required in order for an agency to use an existing piece of music (e.g., a popular record) for a television commercial. It entitles the agency to synchronize the music to visuals. When an outside source of music is used for a radio commercial, it is called a transcription license. This license only gives the licensor the right to rerecord the song—not to use the master recording, which is owned by a record company. The master rights are a separate negotiation. (A master is the actual recording that is owned by the record label.) All sync fees are negotiated; there are no standard rates. The popularity of the copyright determines the value.

> Some composers who write commercials have written commercially successful records. It is not unusual for an agency to contact that composer to license his song and have him adapt it for a commercial. Hire an experienced negotiator to negotiate the sync or transcription license. The rights can become very complicated and negotiation requires an expert.
>
> The sync and/or transcription fees are in addition to the arranging and production fees due the composer or music company. Do not agree to one fee. Try to negotiate the exclusive right to do all subsequent arrangements of your song for that commercial campaign. This is a difficult concession to get, but worth mentioning.

Society of European Stage Authors and Composers (SEASAC)

SEASAC, the smallest of the three organizations, is the only performing rights organization that is for profit. SEASAC has a subdivision called SEASAC Latina that collects for Spanish-language music.

Managing a music house: the following is my interview with John Russo, president of Russo/Grantham Productions, a commercial music house in New York City:

Question: "How can a young person start a music company?"

Russo: "Usually, it's extremely difficult to just hang up a shingle and declare yourself a music company and go out and solicit business successfully. Our business is known for having personal relationships, and it's very rare, if not impossible, to start off cold not knowing anybody as a potential client and winning business. Now, there are lots of different places to bring your work and try to get started. Usually the smallest of advertising agencies on a regional basis are your best bet—but it's the same as any other business—what comes first, the chicken or the egg? You need to get work to show people to get more work. If you have no work to show, you're virtually closed out of anyone giving you the opportunity to do work. My best advice is that if a person really feels as if they would like to be in their own company, they have no choice but to work for an established business first. In other words, you are going to have to do one, two, or three years of dues-paying and work for an established company before you can even get a chance to understand how the business works. The business works a lot on relationship building. The first thing that I would think about is taking existing commercials right off the air and doing my own track. In other words, doing spec work." (John suggests that the composer call the agency and ask if she can do another music track to their commercial.) "If you work in smaller markets, they might take you up on it. After that, what you would hope for if you have demonstrated enough capability is that they would give you a chance to do another spec track for a real job. In other words, to a storyboard or a rough cut. You will have to be doing a series of free demos and have to get familiar or somewhat acquainted with the producer on the job and or the creatives, the copywriter or the art director, and best of all the creative director . . . there are a lot of people vying for a little work. You've got to be imaginative; you've got to be committed, very dedicated to the fact that you know you are going to have to prove yourself before you get a chance to do anything. Now, the flip side of that is that once you have been doing this body of spec work, you're creating your own reel. It's just an ongoing onslaught of making phone calls and diligence—you'll hopefully get an opportunity to work on a real job and have a chance of getting something on air at the time."

Question: "Whom do you negotiate with at an advertising agency?"

Russo: "We deal primarily with the producer and/or the business affairs manager . . . you have to abide by a work-for-hire contract. In other words, the client will own all rights and entitlements to that piece of music. You're basically writing as a supplier—a vendor to this particular agency for this particular product, and you have to assign all right and title. It all comes down to what the budget is and usually it's for the United States and Canada. If the agency elects to use the work in Europe, Asia, or Mexico, or for additional medium rights, let's say radio or Internet, you could negotiate and include that within your budget."

Question: "Are there any instances when you refuse to compete for a job?"

Russo: "Usually, you have to know the landscape of the job. If the creative assignment is something you know is not your strength—let's say, you're an orchestral writer and they want a pop jingle, it really won't make sense for you to write a pop jingle, if your strength is elsewhere because you're going to have a really hard time winning. Also, the demo fees never really cover the expenses involved in producing a demo. So, you're going to lose money, and you're going to have a very remote chance of winning."

Question: "When devising your budget, do you separate your demo fees from your studio and technical fees?"

Russo: "Absolutely . . . usually the writer that wins will get a split of fifty-fifty or sixty-forty (forty for the writer) on the creative fee, plus that writer will try to sing on the commercial and participate as a musician on the commercial. So, they will get three avenues of compensation."

Question: "If the assignment is to write an arrangement of an existing composition, is there still a creative fee or only an arranging fee?"

Russo: "Usually, if there is [only] an arrangement involved, you are allowed to charge what is called a producer's fee. A producer's fee can be anywhere from a quarter to a third to a half of a creative fee, depending upon how much the producer has to work with the arranger."

Question: "What percentage of the time do the agencies allow you to charge a producer's fee?"

Russo: "Whenever there is an arranging job and there is no creative fee."

Question: "What do you do if the creatives are pushing the composer to almost plagiarize an existing composition?"

Russo: "I won't do the job. I have a strict policy about that. Lots of time agencies have a kind of idea about what they'd like and at times give us directions that have elements of songs preexisting in them. We don't mind having that as a direction finder but we do mind when an agency requests us to rip off, so to speak, that person's work, whoever it is. We have a policy where a musicologist is involved in assessing the work we've done to make sure that it has legal clearances. If an agency asks us to change something that is too reminiscent of the original work, we refuse to do it. You've got to stand your ground and say no, because the agency, at times, will not be guided by prudence when they really have made up their mind about something they want and can't have. You have to give them as close to what you believe is safe and with a musicologist's blessing what is possible, but anything after that you have to decline."

Question: "I've seen contracts where the music house is responsible for plagiarism. What do you do to protect yourself from that responsibility?"

Russo: "Basically, what you have to do is have an indemnity clause in your contract that fits your comfort level. Indemnity clause means that you will be responsible for a track only up until what level of litigation you are in. In other words, when we sign an indemnity clause we like to include the phrase 'finally sustained in a court of law,' which means that we are not responsible for any possible infringement up until it's finally sustained, which means going up to the Supreme Court, if necessary. Honestly, the best way to stay clear of that is to know that you shouldn't be close to something to begin with."

Question: "Since demos cost the music company money, what percentage of the jobs that you compete for do you have to win in order to make that investment prudent?"

Russo: "Typically, with a jingle demo, you are doing really good if you can win one in three. Typically, a company or person will win one of five or six, and that's a good company. It's not so much how good you are or how much better the next guy is—it's a question of whose track really seems to reach into the creative direction that's most endearing to the creatives. So it's a very subjective process, and you can't let it get you down if you lose a demo. You have to understand that you've done the best job you could and that, frankly, you have followed the assignment and you'd love to hear what won. On an underscore side, you need to win one of three or four to be able to stay in business. Jingles carry a premium in creative fees—triple that of an underscore—so you could afford to lose more underscores, because they don't cost as much to make. Jingles, you have to really know that you're placing your bets, in that you don't want to be involved unless you know you have a really good chance of winning, which is a one in six, let's say—I mean anything more than five or six music companies I think is too scattered and honestly not necessarily a bona fide job. It may be more of a hunting expedition, and even if you won, would result in a final. So you could win and lose by being involved in the wrong job. Typically, we win over 50 percent of our demo submissions for underscores, and we win about one in four to one in three of our jingles."

Question: "On average, how many demos do you submit on a job?"

Russo: "On an average, we give a minimum of three and a maximum of five. We are trying to show that we are being sensitive to different aspects of the assignment and we want to include as much as possible in the overall presentation."

Question: "Are there any words of advice that you would like to give to people who would like to manage this type of business?"

Russo: "I would not shy away from the other side of the fence and try to work on the agency side. I think that for you to get to know the animal you are trying to wrestle with, you are better to know it from within than from the outside. My best advice would be that instead of trying to trudge up and down Madison Avenue looking for work as an outside supplier, I would rather put together a very nice resume and some good thought put in introductory letters that really go to the point of how you would like to be involved as an employee and a part of the actual industry itself. This way, you can get a job as an assistant producer, you can get a job in business affairs, you can get a job as an administrator, you can get a job in contract law assisting—basically an apprentice-type situation—you could actually make some money, rather than making no money, and you can learn the workings of the mechanics within an agency and actually take that as a three-prong initiative. Number one, you'll be earning, number two, you'll be learning, and number three, you'll be in a position to understand better how to create your best opportunity for yourself ongoing in a later stage of your career development."

Question: "How involved do you get in the creative end of the business?"

Russo: "I get involved to a point where I understand the overall scope of the assignment, the overall direction of the assignment, the overall budgetary allowances of the assignment, the schedule, and the players who are involved. After that, it is more my partner and the creative director who run the actual jingle creations or demo submissions. I have found that you can't be both things in this business and do them both well. In other words, my caveat is don't be an artist thinking that you're going to be an artist and a business affairs executive and vice versa. It's very hard to do sales and run a job from an administrative point of view when your job is already demanding from a creative point of view. So what happens is that one will suffer. Whichever that one is, is the one you don't pay enough attention too. So, if you don't do enough of your homework in making sure you're work is excellent, then you are not going to get a next job, because you are going to lose—and if you are spending too much time on the creative, you are not going to have a chance to get a leg up on what your next assignment is going to be, because you are too busy doing the job you already have. So, there has to be a separate, divide and conquer-type message that one person cannot be all things to this business."

Question: "Is there anything else you would like to say?"

Russo: "My best advice is to follow your heart. However you feel and whatever makes your soul want to be involved in the creative side, what is really the business of selling products is how you should approach what you do. We are in a unique position where we employ art to sell merchandise . . . it's as much a business point of view as it is creative."

CONCLUSION

It is prudent for any composer to understand the business of advertising. It is wise to use experts, for example, attorneys, accountants, musicologists, and union experts, to counsel composers and music companies. Remember the following:

1. When dealing with unions, adhere to all of their rules.
2. When there is any question about possible plagiarism, have the agency employ the services of a musicologist.
3. If there is any confusion with the agency contract, hire an attorney who specializes in advertising.

ASSIGNMENTS

1. You have started a new music house that specializes in commercials. How are you going to market your new venture? Write a marketing plan.
2. Construct a budget for a local commercial. Call the local agencies to find out what average fees are in your market and proceed with writing a budget.

Conclusion

Popular music reflects contemporary culture, and so does most advertising. Composing for commercials is not necessarily a stepping-stone to composing for films or television. It is a highly developed and specialized craft on its own. Advertising music serves several purposes:

1. It helps to "sew" the commercial together by creating the proper mood and emphasizing important information.
2. A jingle becomes entertainment and delivers a message through lyrics.

Many performers only work on jingles. The field is challenging and creative and should be studied as a separate subject; others specialize in underscoring and are generally excellent arrangers and orchestrators.

For students to gain the most from this book, they should purchase a computer sequencing program that contains digital audio and a graphics card that enables them to load video footage. In addition, they should have a number of basic synthesizers that will enable them to produce adequate MIDI sounds or samples. This will help students learn the technical process of scoring to film in a much shorter period of time than the periodic use of a school lab.

This craft can only be learned though practical experience.

The student should tape commercials from television and radio and then score them as exercises. Write down the dialogue and rerecord it onto a CD or cassette (with your voice). Load your voice onto a computer sequencing program that is running in sync with the video; then turn off the sound on the original commercial and begin composing while listening to yourself and viewing the commercial simultaneously. This should become a routine procedure for practicing. (If you do not have a video capture card that enables you to load the video into the computer program, it will be necessary to go to a studio and have an SMPTE time code put on one of the tracks of the video and burn a visual time code on the screen.)

Compose two or three completely different pieces, in different styles, for each commercial.

Theory must be applied.

Composing should always be approached from an emotional viewpoint rather than from an intellectual perspective. One's intellect should only be used to figure out the mechanics of composing to film, analyzing the film, and the placement of music. Other than that, the process should be creative.

The following are quotes by Dale Johnson, who is a writer and creative director at Creative Advertising Solutions in New York City:

"Music is often remembered after the words are gone."

"The right music can be attention getting, motivating, and memorable."

"Music is so powerful, it doesn't need words."

"Music helps tell you what to feel and how to feel it."

"Music can move people emotionally even when the advertising is rational."

"Music reaches the emotional side of a person that no rational argument can."

"Think how scary music can make you feel; that shows how music reaches deep inside you."

"Music reaches into a person where nothing else can go."

The opportunities and the role of the composer in video games, commercials, corporate videos, the Internet, and infomercials are continually expanding. As technology becomes less expensive, opportunities increase because the volume of work increases.

Composing is rewriting—there was only one Mozart!

Index

About the Author

Michael Zager holds the Dorothy F. Schmidt Eminent Scholar Chair in Performing Arts and is professor of music at Florida Atlantic University in Boca Raton, Florida. He previously taught at the Mannes College of Music, a division of New School University in New York City. He is a graduate of the University of Miami and the Mannes College of Music and is a Fulbright senior specialist candidate. In addition, Mr. Zager created the Commercial Music Program at Florida Atlantic University, which won an award for best new major from *Florida Leader* magazine in 2003.

Zager has produced, composed, and/or arranged original music for a wide range of musical idioms, including commercials, albums, network television programs, and major motion pictures.

He has written more than four hundred commercials for clients, including Dr Pepper, MCI, Masterlock, Cablevision, Buick, Acura, IBM, Schlitz Malt Liquor (sung by Kool and the Gang, The Spinners, .38 Special, and the Chi-lites), Bounce (sung by Whitney Houston), Crystal Light (sung by Raquel Welch), Budweiser, Crest, Kodak, Ivory Shampoo, Maxwell House Coffee, Clearasil, Lancôme, Volvo, Burger King, and Oscal (featuring Olympic gold medalist Peggy Fleming).

He has received numerous advertising awards for composing and/or arranging, including a Clio Award, three International Film Festival Awards, three Art Directors Club Awards, and a Mobius Advertising Award. For many years his company has produced The American Advertising Federation Hall of Achievement Awards.

Mr. Zager has produced Grammy Award-winning artists Whitney Houston, Cissy Houston, Peabo Bryson, Luther Vandross, Denise Williams, Jennifer Holliday, Joe Williams, Arturo Sandoval, Herb Alpert, Olatungi, and the Spinners.

His record awards for producing, composing, and/or arranging include thirteen gold or platinum records, Golden Boot Award (France), Europe 1 Award (France), Olé Award (Spain), two BMI Citations of Achievement Awards, given for most-performed songs on radio in a given year, a Grammy Award nomination for "Cupid/I've Loved You for a Long Time," performed by the Spinners, and nomination for Producer of the Year Golden Music Awards in Nashville. He produced Daniel Ray Edwards, who was nominated for Best New Artist Golden Music Awards in Nashville, produced "You Win Again," which was nominated for Single of the Year Golden Music Award in Nashville, and nominated for Best Independent Record Label of the Year for a Golden Music Award in Nashville.

His television awards include a Platinum Video Award for the ABC Television Network series *ABC FUNFIT*, with Mary Lou Retton, and a Daytime Emmy Award for *ABC FUNFIT*, with Mary Lou Retton.